I0797530

# THE O. J. SIMPSON MURDER CASE

By Todd Kortemeier

Content Consultant

Darnell M. Hunt
Dean of Social Sciences
University of California, Los Angeles

AMERICAN CRIME STORIES

An Imprint of Abdo Publishing | abdobooks.com

**ABDOBOOKS.COM**

Published by Abdo Publishing, a division of ABDO, PO Box 398166, Minneapolis, Minnesota 55439. 

Printed in the United States of America, North Mankato, Minnesota.
102019
012020

Cover Photo: Steve Marcus/Reuters/AP Images
Interior Photos: Erika Tcogoeva/Shutterstock Images, 5; Eric Draper/AP Images, 7, 54, 63; Al Messerschmidt/AP Images, 8, 25; Tetiana Ch/Shutterstock Images, 13; Nick Ut/AP Images, 15, 39, 79; Vinnie Zuffante/Archive Photos/Getty Images, 17; Jean-Marc Giboux/Hulton Archive/Getty Images, 23; AP Images, 28, 30, 51; Ron Galella/Ron Galella Collection/Getty Images, 32; Everett Collection/Newscom, 35; Douglas C. Pizac/AP Images, 37; Red Line Editorial, 44; Reed Saxon/AP Images, 46, 49; Sam Microvich/AP Images, 59, 67; Time & Life Pictures/The LIFE Picture Collection/Getty Images, 69; Clark Jones/AP Images, 70; Myung J. Chun/AP Images, 72; Susan Sterner/AP Images, 83; eBay/PacificCoastNews/Newscom, 87; Damian Dovarganes/AP Images, 91; Isaac Brekken/AP Images, 94; Jason Bean/The Reno Gazette-Journal/AP Images, 97

Editor: Charly Haley
Series Designer: Melissa Martin

**LIBRARY OF CONGRESS CONTROL NUMBER: 2019941969**

**PUBLISHER'S CATALOGING-IN-PUBLICATION DATA**

Names: Kortemeier, Todd, author.
Title: The O. J. Simpson murder case / by Todd Kortemeier
Description: Minneapolis, Minnesota: Abdo Publishing, 2020 | Series: American crime stories | Includes online resources and index.
Identifiers: ISBN 9781532190131 (lib. bdg) | ISBN 9781532175985 (ebook)
Subjects: LCSH: Simpson, O. J., 1947- (Orenthal James Simpson)--Juvenile literature. | Killing (Murder)--Juvenile literature. | Trials (Murder)--California--Los Angeles--Juvenile literature. | Criminal justice, Administration of--Juvenile literature. | Homicide--Juvenile literature. | Simpson, Nicole Brown, 1959-1994--Juvenile literature.
Classification: DDC 364.152--dc23

# CONTENTS

CHAPTER ONE
THE DOG WITH BLOODY PAWS 4

CHAPTER TWO
O.J. ON THE RUN 14

CHAPTER THREE
FOOTBALL AND MARRIAGE 24

CHAPTER FOUR
THE ROLE OF RACE 34

CHAPTER FIVE
THE TRIAL BEGINS 48

CHAPTER SIX
THE GLOVE DOESN'T FIT 58

CHAPTER SEVEN
THE VERDICT 68

CHAPTER EIGHT
THE LAWSUIT 78

CHAPTER NINE
SIMPSON GOES TO PRISON 86

Timeline 98
Essential Facts 100
Glossary 102
Additional Resources 104
Source Notes 106
Index 110
About the Author 112

CHAPTER ONE

# THE DOG WITH BLOODY PAWS

The Brentwood neighborhood in Los Angeles, California, was quiet as usual on the evening of June 12, 1994. Brentwood is far away from the hustle and bustle of Hollywood and downtown Los Angeles. Many stars live there, considering it a quiet retreat from the world.

The silence late that evening was disrupted by the sound of a barking dog. It startled neighbors on South Bundy Drive. Pablo Fenjves was at home watching the ten o'clock news. He heard what he called a "plaintive wail" coming from the alley that ran behind his apartment.[1] Another neighbor, Eva Stein, was awakened by the sound. She was unable to go back to sleep.

Steven Schwab was walking his own dog late that night. It was getting close to 11:00 p.m. When he came to the corner of Dorothy Street and South Bundy Drive, he saw a dog standing

**A barking dog was the first sign that something was wrong in Brentwood on June 12, 1994.**

in the middle of the street. From a distance, Schwab thought the dog was dirty and needed a bath. But as he got closer, he saw the dog's paws and legs were covered in blood.

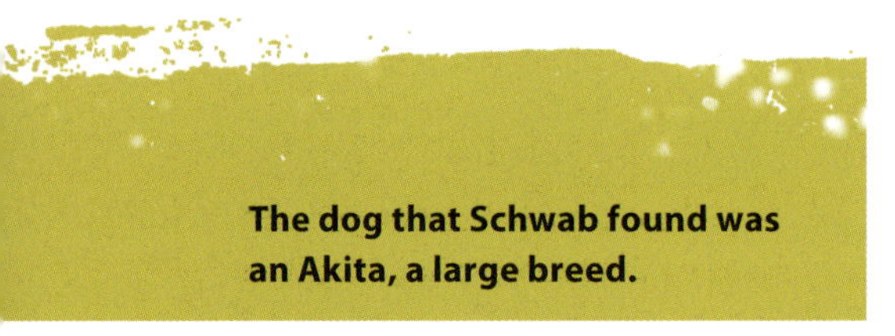
**The dog that Schwab found was an Akita, a large breed.**

The dog was not hurt. The blood must have come from somewhere else. And it was still wet, meaning whatever happened had happened recently. Schwab turned to go to his house two and one-half blocks away. But the dog followed him. He gave the dog a bowl of water while he figured out what to do.

Schwab thought about taking the dog to an animal shelter. But instead, he went back out with the dog on a leash to find out where it lived. As they got closer to the spot where Schwab had found the dog, the dog began to act strangely. It was nervous and did not want to walk any farther. "It was not allowing me to walk it towards Bundy," Schwab later said.[2]

So Schwab returned home with the dog, unsure of what to do next. At about 11:40, Schwab's neighbor Sukru Boztepe came home. Boztepe offered to keep the dog until they could find its owner in the morning. But seeing how upset the dog was, Boztepe and his wife chose to walk the dog back to Bundy in another attempt to find its owner.

It was nearly midnight when they were walking up South Bundy Drive. The dog began pulling on its leash and getting more and more upset. It stopped right as they got to house number 875. The dog looked toward the house, and Boztepe looked the same way. "I saw a lot of blood," he said. "I turned to my wife and said that was a dead person there."[3]

## O. J. Simpson

Approximately two miles (3.2 km) away, in a house on Rockingham Avenue, struggling actor Kato Kaelin was resting that night. He was staying in the guesthouse of ex–football star O. J. Simpson. Kaelin was startled at about 10:40 p.m. by the sound of three thumps against the wall of the guesthouse. At first, he thought it was an earthquake. Later, he described

After police heard about the death at 875 South Bundy Drive, the house was blocked off as a crime scene for investigation.

it as the sound of someone falling. Kaelin went outside to investigate, but he didn't see anyone around the house. He did see a limousine driver outside the front gate.

The driver, Allan Park, was there to take Simpson to the airport. He called and called for Simpson using the house's intercom, but there was no response. Just before 11:00 p.m., Park called his office to say nobody was home. But he was told to wait. Simpson was always running late. Just a few minutes later, Park saw someone enter the house from the driveway.

Finally, there was an answer on the intercom. Simpson said he had overslept and simply had to shower and would be down shortly. At about 11:15, Simpson put his bags into the limo, and

Despite retiring from football in 1979, O. J. Simpson was still a beloved celebrity in the early 1990s.

he and Park headed for the airport. Simpson caught his flight to Chicago, which departed around 11:45.

## KATO KAELIN

Simpson's houseguest, Kato Kaelin, became something of a minor celebrity due to his association with Simpson. Kaelin was a struggling actor living in Los Angeles in the early 1990s. He was divorced and had a daughter he was trying to raise alone on very little money. He had only a few acting credits to his name, mostly in small roles.

Kaelin happened to meet Simpson's then-wife, Nicole Brown Simpson, while on a trip to Aspen, Colorado, in 1992. Wanting to help, she offered Kaelin the guesthouse at the Simpson home as a place to live. Kaelin became a family friend and also babysat the Simpson children. Kaelin and O. J. Simpson remained friends even after the Simpsons divorced.

## A River of Blood

Police Officer Robert Riske got a call just after midnight. It was a report of an unknown person ringing the doorbell of a home across the street from 875 South Bundy Drive. As Riske pulled up to the house, two people with a dog flagged him down. They were the unknown people who had rung the doorbell. They were trying to get help. They told Riske they had just seen a dead woman at 875 South Bundy.

Riske shined his flashlight across the walkway of the house. There, he saw a blond woman in a black dress lying on the ground, dead. After calling for backup, Riske and his partner investigated further and found the body of a man just two feet away. The sidewalk was covered in blood that flowed down to the street like a river. In the blood were occasional paw prints from the victim's dog.

There were also potential key pieces of evidence. Officers found a glove and a ski cap completely soaked in blood. There were footprints in the blood, too. Nothing appeared missing from the home. It did not appear to be a robbery gone wrong. It looked as if whoever killed these people had come to the house specifically to kill them.

The home belonged to Nicole Brown Simpson, the ex-wife of O. J. Simpson. Her two children were sleeping upstairs. She was the dead woman in the black dress. The dead man was her friend, Ronald Goldman. How they ended up there was a monumental mystery. But detectives had a hunch about where to start putting the pieces together. Brown's ex-husband lived close by.

### RONALD GOLDMAN

Ronald Goldman was born in Chicago and moved to Los Angeles in 1987 when he was 18. While pursuing a modeling and acting career, he worked part-time jobs like the serving job he had at the time of the murders. Friends remembered him as a kind young man who loved life and was always on the lookout for his next big adventure. He and Brown had become good friends in the 18 months leading up to the killings. Goldman was 25 when he died.

## Nobody Home

Detectives arrived at the O. J. Simpson estate at around 5:00 a.m. on June 13. Getting no answer on the intercom, the officers chose to hop over the house's fence. Searching a property usually requires a search warrant signed by a judge, but these were extreme circumstances. Police said they did not know if Simpson was safe after his ex-wife had been killed. The killer who targeted her may have gone after him.

Police confirmed there was nobody at the house. But they found something else, too. There were bloodstains on the driveway, and there was a bloodstain on the door of Simpson's white Ford Bronco.

## THE PITCHMAN

Simpson had been retired from the National Football League (NFL) for 15 years by the time of the murders. But he was still well known thanks to a career on television, acting and promoting products. One of Simpson's most famous appearances was as the pitchman for Hertz, a car rental company. In fact, Simpson was headed to a Hertz conference in Chicago the night of the murders.

Simpson started doing commercials for Hertz toward the end of his NFL career. The commercials were incredibly successful, as the company reported a profit increase of 50 percent.[4] Most of the ads featured Simpson using his football skills to run through the airport to get to a Hertz counter.

His success on camera led to more formal acting roles in film and television. Simpson also won awards for Star Presenter of the Year by the advertising magazine *Ad Age*. Simpson's relationship with Hertz ended after the 1994 murders.

Detectives were able to reach Simpson by phone after he arrived in Chicago. They informed him that his ex-wife had been found dead. "Oh my God," he said, "Nicole was killed.

Nicole is dead."[5] Simpson kept repeating that over and over. Detectives noted this as strange. Many people who have lost a loved one have questions. They want to know how it happened, and why. They are in shock. Simpson's reaction did not make him a suspect, but detectives thought it was unusual.

## BRENTWOOD

Brentwood is known as a quiet, very wealthy neighborhood of Los Angeles. It was not where one would expect to find a double murder. Before the murders of Nicole Brown Simpson and Ronald Goldman, the neighborhood was most famous for the site of the Bel Air Fire that destroyed nearly 500 homes in 1961.[6] O. J. Simpson bought his Rockingham Avenue house in 1977. Many other celebrities have lived in Brentwood over the years, such as New England Patriots quarterback Tom Brady and LeBron James of the Los Angeles Lakers.

While at the house, police also talked to Kaelin. He told them about the thumps he heard in the night. That led the investigators to look behind the guesthouse. There, they made a shocking discovery. They found a bloody glove. It looked like an exact match to the one found on South Bundy Drive.

Police Detective Philip Vannatter declared Simpson's house a crime scene. He went to obtain a warrant to legally search the property. And O. J. Simpson was on a flight back to Los Angeles to face questioning. Though police felt they already had some answers, the full picture was only beginning to take shape.

# THE CRIME SCENES

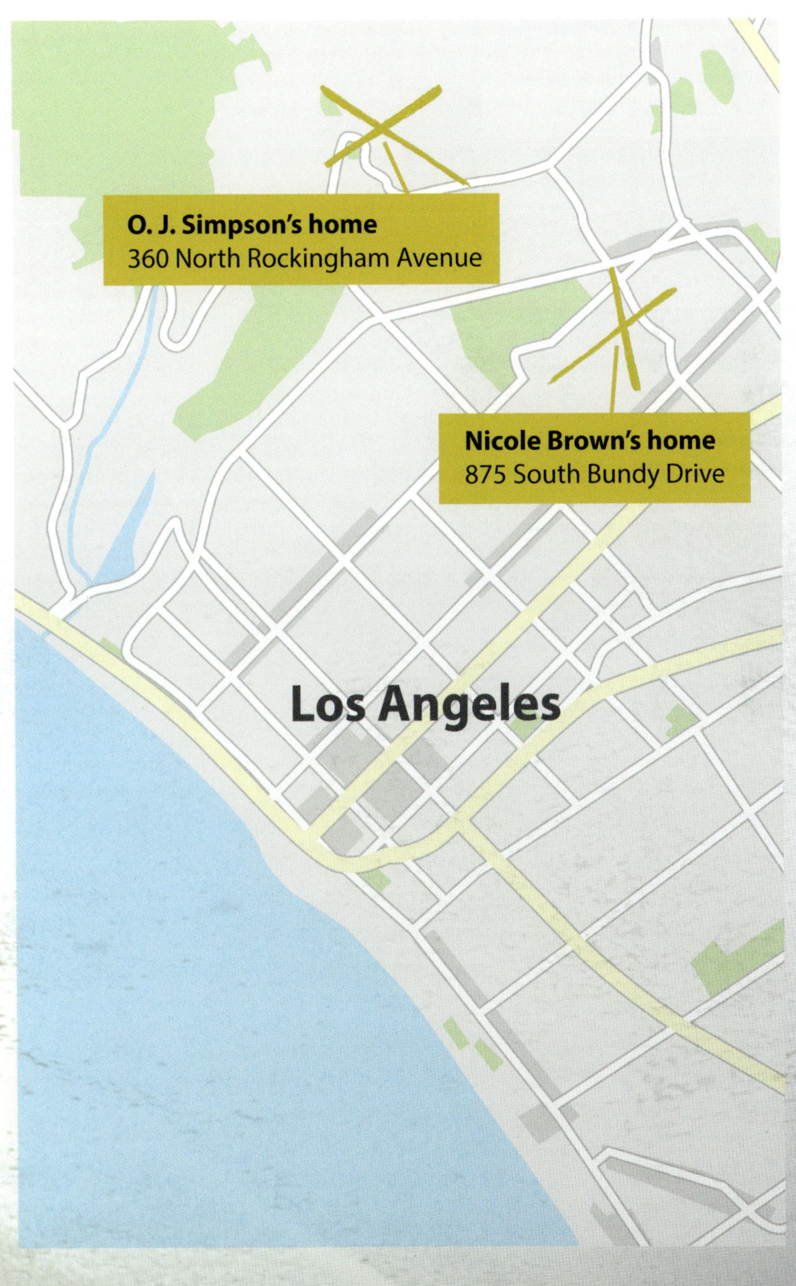

CHAPTER TWO

# O.J. ON THE RUN

After hearing about his ex-wife's death, Simpson caught the first flight from Chicago to Los Angeles. But that was not the first thing he did. From his Chicago hotel, he made a phone call. He arranged to have a lawyer meet him at his Rockingham estate. At this time, detectives had not informed Simpson that his ex-wife had been murdered, only that she had been found dead.

Simpson arrived back at Rockingham at approximately 12:10 p.m. on June 13. Waiting for him were officers from the Los Angeles Police Department (LAPD) and a swarm of reporters and photographers. One officer mistakenly put handcuffs on Simpson, even though he had not been arrested. Simpson was soon released, but not soon enough for one photographer, who, by reaching above Simpson's fence, got a

**Simpson sits in his lawyer's car after being questioned by police on June 13, 1994.**

photo of the beloved football hero in handcuffs. The photo was printed in newspapers around the world.

Detectives had already noted the blood around the Simpson property. That detail became even more suspicious when they saw a cut on Simpson's left hand. The droplets of blood at the murder scene were found to the left of shoe prints, indicating they came from the left side of the killer's body. Detectives wanted to question Simpson about this and more. Simpson agreed to answer their questions.

Simpson spoke with detectives for hours. They asked him about his whereabouts on the night of the murders. Simpson said he had attended his daughter's dance recital and then went home. He mentioned trying to reach his girlfriend and going out for dinner with Kaelin, but detectives Vannatter and Thomas Lange never established an exact timeline of when these events occurred.

They also asked Simpson about the cut on his hand. Simpson said he had cut it on a glass in his hotel room in Chicago, but also that it had been cut before. Vannatter and Lange never got Simpson to commit to one version of the story. Prosecutors later criticized the detectives for not establishing this important point, because Simpson had no concrete alibi for the time of the murders. The detectives told Simpson about the

News reporters gathered outside Simpson's home, seeking more information about Brown's murder.

blood they had found. Simpson said if it was from him, then it came from his haste in packing for his trip to Chicago.

Simpson never provided any clear explanations for several of the unknowns in the case. After three hours of questioning, Simpson was released. He was not arrested. The LAPD did not declare Simpson a suspect at that time, but he was the focus of the investigation. LAPD investigators were combing through the evidence.

Investigators first wanted to test the blood found at the crime scene. They had to compare it with the blood found at Simpson's home. The samples were a match for the same type. That meant it was not certain it was Simpson's blood specifically, but it seemed unlikely the samples would have come from different people. Given all the evidence, a warrant was issued for Simpson's arrest.

## "Mr. Simpson Is Out There"

O. J. Simpson was charged with murder on the morning of June 17. The LAPD called Simpson's lawyer, Robert Shapiro, and told him to turn Simpson in. Shapiro arranged for his client to turn himself in that morning, at 11:00.

Shapiro met with Simpson at 9:30 a.m. He told him about the 11:00 a.m. deadline. But then the deadline came and went with no sign of Simpson.

After noon, detectives got tired of waiting. They dispatched several police cars to the house where they knew Simpson was staying. When they arrived, they learned that Simpson had left some time earlier. This made the situation even more serious for the police. Simpson was now considered a fugitive.

"Mr. Simpson is out there somewhere," said Police Commander David Gascon in a press conference. "And we will find him."[1] Police identified some areas they thought Simpson might run to, such as the grave of his ex-wife, who had been buried just days earlier. They also knew the car Simpson would be in, a white Ford Bronco. It was nearly identical to the one on which detectives found blood, but this car belonged to Simpson's friend and former football teammate, Al "A. C." Cowlings, who was the driver. A warrant was also issued for Cowlings's arrest.

At about 5:00 p.m., Simpson called a press conference. Simpson's longtime friend Robert Kardashian, an attorney who would later join Simpson's legal team, spoke at the press conference, urging Simpson to turn himself in. He also read a note Simpson had written sometime before his disappearance. In the note, Simpson said he was innocent. He wrote, "Don't feel sorry for me. I've had a great life, great friends. Please think of the real O. J. and not this lost person."[2]

Many who heard the note believed Simpson was planning to kill himself. More of Simpson's

**Cowlings and Simpson were born weeks apart in 1947 in San Francisco. Both played football at the University of Southern California (USC) and in the NFL for the Bills and 49ers. Cowlings was a defensive player.**

## KEPT UP WITH THE KARDASHIANS

The O. J. Simpson case was the first time many Americans heard the name Kardashian. Robert Kardashian was Simpson's friend and lawyer. Although both men had attended USC, they didn't become friends until the 1970s. By the time of the murders, Kardashian had stopped practicing law and was a businessman. But he renewed his license to help Simpson with his legal defense. Kardashian and wife Kris had four children: Kourtney, Kim, Khloe, and Rob. Robert Kardashian died in 2003, but his ex-wife and children went on to star in the reality TV series *Keeping Up with the Kardashians*. Simpson was a family friend while the Kardashian children were young.

friends urged him to surrender. His old college football coach, John McKay, went on a local radio station and said, "We love you Juice," which was Simpson's football nickname. "Just pull over," McKay said, "and I'll come out and stand by you all the rest of my life."[3]

## "There's a White Bronco!"

Chris Thomas and Kathy Ferrigno were on their way to go camping on the evening of June 17. The couple had seen the news report of Simpson's disappearance earlier in the day. The report had included the license plate number of Cowlings's Bronco. Thomas wrote it down just in case. At around 6:25 p.m., as Thomas and Ferrigno were driving north on Interstate 5, they found themselves in the middle of the chase.

"Chris! Chris! Chris! There's a white Bronco!" Ferrigno said.[4] Thomas got behind the Bronco and checked the license plate number. The vehicle's license plate matched the number reported on the news. Thomas and Ferrigno called the police. Within minutes, cop cars were speeding toward the Bronco in hopes of ending the search for Simpson.

The chase was on, but very slowly. Police followed the Bronco, driven by Cowlings, at about 35 miles per hour (56 kmh). In a call to police, Cowlings seemed to confirm the suicidal intentions from Simpson's note. Cowlings said he was taking Simpson to see his mother, and that the police should back off. Simpson was holding a gun to his own head.

## AT SLOW SPEED

The route traveled during the Bronco chase used some of Los Angeles's busiest freeways, and it happened at the end of the evening rush hour. Interstate 405, also known as the San Diego Freeway, is considered the busiest and most-congested freeway in the United States. Nearly 400,000 vehicles use it every day.[6] The low-speed chase snarled traffic in the area for the rest of the evening.

## The World Watches

June 17, 1994, was a huge sports day in the United States. The first soccer World Cup ever played on American soil kicked off in Chicago. The New York Rangers held a parade for winning hockey's Stanley Cup. The Houston Rockets and New York Knicks played Game 5 of the National Basketball Association (NBA) Finals. But the biggest sports story of all was that NFL legend O. J. Simpson was on the run, suspected of double murder. During its NBA Finals broadcast, NBC devoted half of the screen to the Simpson chase. All other TV networks showed nonstop coverage of the chase.

Approximately 95 million people watched the chase live on TV.[5] That was more than the audience for that year's NFL Super Bowl. The Simpson chase beat every Super Bowl in ratings until 2008. Pizza delivery chain Domino's reported record sales. People ordered delivery instead of leaving the TV screen to cook dinner. The Simpson case had become a national

## THE BRONCO

Contrary to public belief at the time, the Bronco used in the chase was not Simpson's. It belonged to Cowlings, who wanted to get rid of the famous car as quickly as possible after its infamous trip with Simpson. He sold it to a group that included his lawyer and Simpson's agent. Then the car mostly remained in storage for 17 years, being driven only 20 miles (32 km) in that time. The owners listed the car for sale in 2017. But at a price of more than $1 million, the car didn't sell. The owners later reached a deal to have the car displayed at the East Alcatraz Crime Museum in Pigeon Forge, Tennessee. As of 2019, the car remained in the museum and was not for sale.

obsession. People couldn't imagine that a beloved celebrity like Simpson could be a murderer.

For 45 minutes, people watched as Cowlings's Bronco slowly wound its way through the Los Angeles freeways, followed by police. News helicopters flew overhead. As people saw what was happening on TV, they went outside to be a part of it. Crowds lined overpasses, and people waved to the car. Most seemed to be supporting Simpson. There were cheers of "Go O. J., go!" and people held up encouraging signs.[7] Although he was suspected of double murder, many people had already decided that the charming Simpson was innocent.

It became clear based on the route that Simpson was heading home to Brentwood. Police were already waiting there, along with a crowd of reporters and Simpson's fans. The Bronco slowly made its way through the crowd, then into the driveway.

Simpson's 24-year-old son, Jason, ran out of the house to his father, but Cowlings pushed him away.

Police surrounded the car, knowing Simpson had a gun. For almost an hour, Simpson remained inside the car. Police tried to persuade him to come out. They told him that his children needed him, and that he should come out and clear everything up if he was innocent.

At 8:53 p.m., Simpson stepped out of the Bronco. He was holding some family pictures. Items left behind in the Bronco included a loaded gun, a fake mustache and goatee, and Simpson's passport.

Police led Simpson into the house. "I'm sorry, guys," Simpson said. "I'm sorry I put you through this."[8] After that, Simpson was arrested and taken downtown in a squad car. Once there, he was criminally charged with the murders of Nicole Brown Simpson and Ronald Goldman. The chase was over. But the case was just beginning.

People stopped their cars and lined the streets to cheer for Simpson during the chase.

## CHAPTER THREE

# FOOTBALL AND MARRIAGE

The sight of O. J. Simpson running from the law was stunning to anyone who remembered the runs he used to make as a football player. Simpson was one of the greatest running backs in the history of the NFL. Many people considered the story of how Simpson got to the NFL to be an inspiring example of perseverance.

Simpson was born on July 9, 1947. He grew up in a rough part of San Francisco, California, and at times he was a member of a local street gang. Simpson's parents split up when he was four. He and his siblings were raised mostly by their mother.

As a teenager, Simpson was arrested three times for gang activity. He was involved in numerous fights. But sports became a way for him to stay out of trouble. When Simpson was 17, he got the chance to spend time with San Francisco Giants

**Simpson spent most of his NFL career playing for the Buffalo Bills.**

baseball legend Willie Mays. Mays took Simpson to his home, told him about how much ability he had, and encouraged him to keep out of trouble. The meeting had a profound impact on Simpson. "It was hard to believe," Simpson said later. "I'd seen Willie play ball I don't know how many times. . . . I was saying to myself, 'I'm going to be like him.'"[1]

## SIMPSON'S FATHER

One subject Simpson rarely talked about was his father. Jimmy Lee Simpson was gay, which O. J. Simpson knew from a young age. At the time, being gay was largely not accepted in the African American community, even in a city with a significant gay population like San Francisco. But Simpson maintained a relationship with his father, who attended some of Simpson's major football achievements. Jimmy Simpson died of acquired immunodeficiency syndrome (AIDS) in 1985.

Simpson was a star running back in high school. But he was a poor student. Few colleges recruited him because of his grades, forcing him to attend the tiny City College of San Francisco. After scoring three touchdowns in a win over Long Beach State, Simpson met with a recruiter from the University of Southern California (USC), which was celebrated as one of the nation's premier college football programs. Simpson played two seasons at USC. He led the country in rushing in both 1967 and 1968. He won the Heisman Trophy, given to the best college football player in the country, in 1968. Then, in the 1969 NFL Draft, Simpson was the

No. 1 overall pick, chosen by the Buffalo Bills.

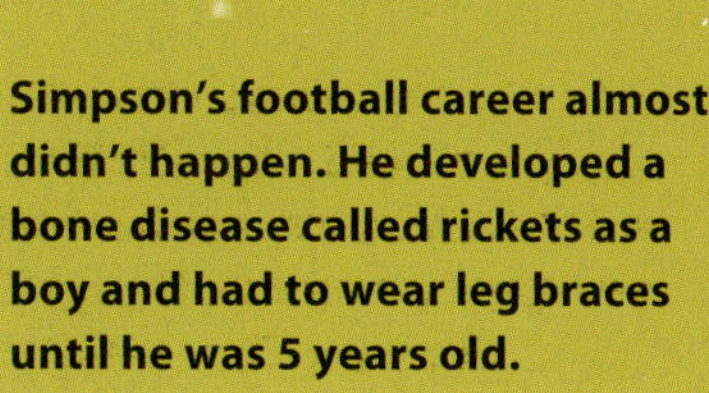

**Simpson's football career almost didn't happen. He developed a bone disease called rickets as a boy and had to wear leg braces until he was 5 years old.**

## Turning On the Juice

Despite Simpson's dominance in college, the Bills did not use him much at first. It was not until Buffalo hired a new coach in 1972 that Simpson started to get more opportunities. He got more than 100 more carries in 1972 than he had in 1971.[2] He had his first 1,000-yard rushing season.

Simpson topped that with a historic year in 1973. He became the first running back in NFL history to rush for more than 2,000 yards. And he did it in only 14 games, compared with the modern 16-game schedule.

The Bills' offensive line was key to Simpson's success. They were nicknamed the "Electric Company" because they "turned on the Juice."[3] Simpson played nine years in Buffalo and two years with his hometown San Francisco 49ers. He retired after the 1979 season with the second-most career rushing yards in NFL history.[4]

## A Chance Meeting

Two years before retiring from the NFL, Simpson had a chance encounter with a waitress at a nightclub in Beverly Hills,

Simpson, while playing for the 49ers, signs an autograph for a young fan.

California. He was 30 and still married to his first wife, Marguerite. They had three children together: Arnelle, Jason, and Aaren. The waitress was 18. Simpson fell in love with her.

Her name was Nicole Brown. She was born on May 19, 1959, in Germany. Her father met her German mother while he was stationed there during his service in the US Air Force. The family eventually settled in Southern California. Brown was well liked. Her friends and family described her as beautiful, strong, and fun-loving. In high school, she was named homecoming princess.

Brown was barely out of high school when she met Simpson. He was a frequent guest of the nightclub, but Brown did not know who he was, not even from his football career. Still, she was drawn to him. The couple moved in together just a few months later. Brown dropped out of community college. Simpson and his wife divorced in 1979.

## MARGUERITE SIMPSON

Simpson was married once before Nicole Brown. Marguerite Whitley and Simpson went to high school together and got married in 1967 when she was 18 and he was 19. The couple had troubles from the beginning, and Whitley nearly filed for divorce as early as 1973. As Simpson became more of a celebrity, their marriage had more problems. They divorced in 1979, the same year the family suffered a tragedy. Their youngest child, Aaren, drowned in the pool at the Rockingham house.

Nicole Brown

## Violence

Friends noticed Brown and Simpson having problems, even before they got married in 1985. Simpson would sometimes throw Brown out of their house. Then he'd call and apologize, and she would go back to him. The Simpsons had a daughter in 1985 and a son in 1988. There were happy days, the couple's friends said, but the bad days got harder to take.

In the early hours of New Year's Day 1989, Brown called police to the house on Rockingham. According to police reports, Brown ran toward the responding officers when they arrived.

"He's going to kill me," she said.[5] Brown was bruised, scratched, and bloodied. Her injuries were severe enough that she had to go to the hospital. This was not the first time officers had been to Rockingham on abuse complaints. Officers had responded to calls eight times before.[6] Simpson himself acknowledged this at the 1989 incident.

"The police have been out here eight times before, and now you're going to arrest me for this?" Simpson told the officers, according to a police report. "This is a family matter. Why do you want to make a big deal out of it when we can handle it?"[7]

It's unclear why Simpson was never arrested on the previous calls. But this time he was arrested and convicted.

## THE HALL OF FAMER

NFL players must wait five years after retirement before they are eligible for the Pro Football Hall of Fame. Simpson was inducted in 1985, in his first year of eligibility. Simpson at the time was one of the best running backs ever. He ranked second in career rushing yards and held the record for most touchdowns in a season with 23. At his Hall of Fame speech, Simpson thanked his then-new wife Nicole. "My wife, Nicole, who came into my life at what is probably the most difficult time for an athlete, at the end of my career," Simpson said to her. "And she turned those years into some of the best years I've had in my life."[8]

In public, Simpson and Brown appeared to have a fun, glamorous relationship.

## DOMESTIC VIOLENCE

Before the news of the murders, many people believed that the Simpsons had a perfect life. They were famous, rich, and attractive. But after Simpson was arrested on suspicion of murdering Brown, the couple's marriage was scrutinized under a national spotlight, publicly revealing the abuse that Simpson had inflicted on Brown. Simpson beat Brown often, and repeated calls to the police had failed to stop it. The Simpson case helped bring public attention to the issue of domestic violence. People realized that this type of abuse could happen to anyone, even to people whose lives appear perfect. While news of the case continued to unfold, domestic violence hotlines and shelters across the country received an increase in calls as people felt empowered to report abuse. "[Brown's] murder hurled into the forefront a conversation that advocates had been having for years—that it could happen anywhere, to anyone," journalist Rachel Louise Snyder wrote.[10]

However, Simpson escaped jail time for the abusive incident. He was sentenced to undergo therapy instead. Simpson picked his own therapist, and they held sessions over the phone.

## The End

Brown filed for divorce in 1992. Friends said they noticed a change in her. She reconnected with some friends she had lost touch with over the years. She even started dating again. Things were looking up.

However, she and Simpson continued to see each other. They even talked about getting remarried. But nothing seemed to change about Simpson's behavior. Brown made a 911 call to the police in October 1993. She said Simpson had come over uninvited and was threatening her. When asked by the 911 dispatcher if Simpson had done this in the past, Brown replied, "Many times."[9]

CHAPTER FOUR

# THE ROLE OF RACE

Los Angeles has long been a setting for civil rights struggles. Often, the LAPD has been at the center of these struggles. In 1965, African American driver Marquette Frye was pulled over on suspicion of reckless driving. A scuffle broke out between Frye and police. A crowd of bystanders soon gathered, as they believed white police officers were unfairly beating Frye. Then fights started between the bystanders and police officers.

The fights exploded into six days of riots in the Watts neighborhood of Los Angeles. The US National Guard had to be called in to try to contain the violence. Thirty-four people died; more than 1,000 were injured, and the riots caused more than $40 million in damage.[1]

While sparked by the Frye incident, the Watts Riots were caused by many factors. They were largely a response to

**Police forcefully drag a young black man out of a damaged store during the Watts Riots.**

MASK
GLASS
GLASS

how black people had been treated in the city for decades. Sixty-five black people had been shot by police in the two years before the riots. Twenty-five of them were unarmed.[2] And police leadership did not seem willing to address the issue. Longtime LAPD Commissioner William Parker described the rioters as "monkeys in a zoo."[3]

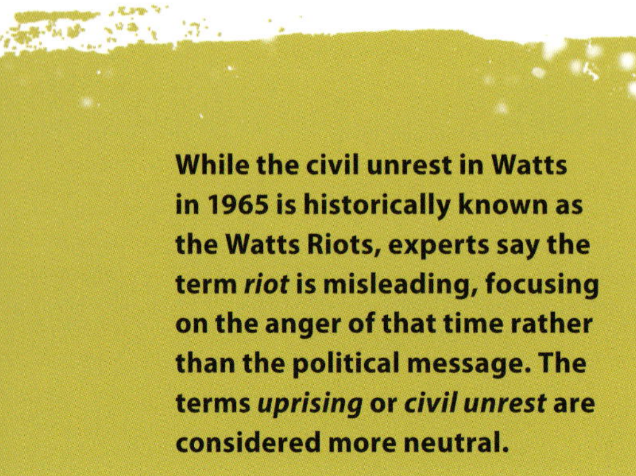

**While the civil unrest in Watts in 1965 is historically known as the Watts Riots, experts say the term *riot* is misleading, focusing on the anger of that time rather than the political message. The terms *uprising* or *civil unrest* are considered more neutral.**

This conflict between the African American community and the LAPD played a significant role in how people saw the O. J. Simpson case. In the years between the Watts Riots and Simpson's arrest, more high-profile incidents of police brutality against black people occurred in Los Angeles. Memories of these incidents were still fresh in the minds of L.A. residents at the time of the Simpson case.

## Deepening Divide

Eulia Love was late paying her gas bill in January 1979. After a confrontation with Love, an employee from the gas company called police. What happened next is unclear, but police shot Love to death at point-blank range. Citizens were appalled when Police Chief Daryl Gates claimed the officers who killed Love were just as much the victims as she was.

In 1982, the LAPD noticed a rise in deaths by officers administering a choke hold. A choke hold is a method that police sometimes use to subdue a suspect by cutting off his or her oxygen supply with an arm around his or her neck. The move had killed 16 people. Twelve of them were black. Gates again gave a controversial explanation: "We may be finding that in some blacks when it is applied, the veins or arteries do not open up as fast as they do on normal people."[4] Gates refused to apologize for this racist comment. Later that year, the

Los Angeles police arrest people as part of a drug bust in April 1988.

Los Angeles city government banned police from using these deadly choke holds.

Then, in August 1988, police were called to an apartment building in South Central Los Angeles. It was part of a police initiative called Operation Hammer, which aimed to get as many drugs and drug dealers off the streets as possible by force. Police believed there were drugs at the South Central apartment. Officers kicked down doors, held citizens at gunpoint, and destroyed the homes and property within. The raid caused so much damage to the apartments that 22 residents were displaced. The officers found a small amount of drugs—less than six ounces of marijuana and less than an ounce of cocaine.[5]

## Rodney King

Outrage on the scale of the Watts Riots returned three years later. An African American man named Rodney King was pulled over for speeding. Despite the relatively minor offense, 21 officers were eventually called to the scene. Three of them beat King with clubs while the rest watched.

The incident happened to be captured on video by a bystander who was recording from a nearby apartment. The video was sold to a TV station and made headlines around the world. The officers were charged with police brutality. They went on trial the next year.

People protest the Rodney King verdict in front of the Los Angeles Police Department.

On April 29, 1992, all of the officers were found not guilty. Within minutes, protesters took to the streets. Rioting began in South Los Angeles, spread to other parts of the city, and lasted for three days. People set buildings on fire, robbed stores, and smashed windows.

The National Guard and the US Marines stepped in to help on May 2. The city slowly got back under control by the following day. Sixty-three people died, and 2,000 were injured in what had become the United States' most costly urban uprising.[6] Gates resigned in June. The city released an investigative report about its own police practices in October.

The investigation determined that the LAPD was slow to respond to and unprepared to handle the civil unrest.

## Trying a Case in Los Angeles

Race played a crucial role in the Simpson case from the beginning. The first major decision in the case was where to file charges. The crime took place near Santa Monica. That would have been the natural place to file charges and try the case in court.

But Los Angeles County District Attorney Gil Garcetti chose to try the case in downtown Los Angeles. He gave several reasons for this. One was that the Santa Monica Courthouse had recently suffered earthquake damage. The building was too small, and the downtown courthouse had just been renovated.

Also, Garcetti thought the verdict would be viewed as less legitimate

### JURY TRIALS

For serious crimes in the United States, the accused (defendant) faces a trial by a jury of his or her peers. A jury pool is assembled from people who live in the area where the case is being tried. Lawyers for both sides of the case are allowed to ask the jurors questions. They want to get a sense of whether potential jurors have any biases that might affect their ability to view the case fairly. Each side gets to reject a certain number of jurors. Once the jury is chosen, the case goes to trial. Each side presents its evidence, and then the jury votes. In most cases, all jurors must agree on the verdict. If they cannot, then the case may have to be tried again.

in Santa Monica. Mostly white, rich people lived there. These residents would make up a Santa Monica jury. That background would likely inform their perspective on the case, and it probably would be easier to get a conviction in Santa Monica. But Garcetti felt that if a Santa Monica jury found Simpson guilty, opponents would call the verdict racist. The backlash could be similar to that of the Rodney King verdict, which was decided by an all-white jury.

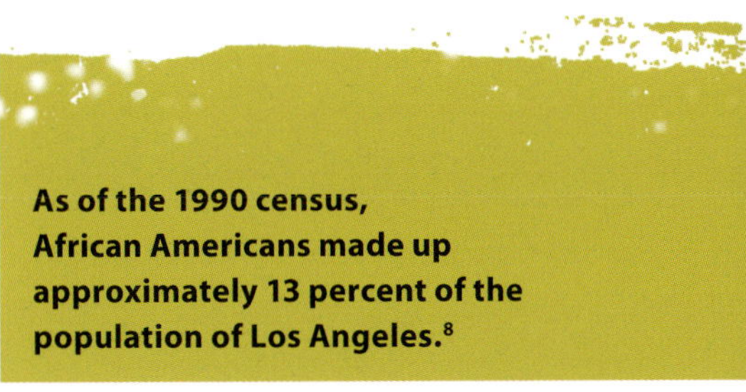

**As of the 1990 census, African Americans made up approximately 13 percent of the population of Los Angeles.[8]**

A downtown jury would be more diverse. Garcetti felt that the Simpson case was so strong, it did not matter where the case was tried. He was confident that Simpson would be convicted.

Although the role of race was heavily considered by both the prosecution and Simpson's defense team, Simpson himself often avoided the subject. Throughout his career, he had largely refrained from talking about his race. To some, it appeared he tried to have people not see him as black or any race, because he did not want to face the discrimination that came with it. Sociologist Harry Edwards, who is black, said of Simpson, "His sentiments were, 'I'm not black, I'm O.J.'"[7] In a time when other black athletes were famously protesting

American race relations, Simpson stood out to many people as an apolitical, feel-good figure. For this reason, he was enormously popular, before the murders, with white Americans.

### THE *TIME* COVER

The issue of race touched every part of the Simpson case. When Simpson's mug shot was made public after his arrest, it made headlines around the world. It was on the cover of both *Newsweek* and *Time* magazine. But the way *Time* treated the cover raised controversy. The picture was made a lot darker than the actual photo. This made Simpson look as if he had darker skin. People said it made black people look more menacing.

## Picking a Jury

During jury selection—a courtroom process in which jurors are chosen after being questioned by the judge and lawyers—it became clear that race was only part of the issue. Prosecutors miscalculated how jurors would feel about certain facts of the case. The prosecutors even ignored the advice of jury consultants concerning the complicated role that race and gender might play in how jurors interpreted the evidence of the Simpson case.

One of the key points the prosecution wanted to make was that Simpson had assaulted Brown repeatedly. Prosecutors thought having women on the jury was key to proving this point. All women would be horrified by domestic violence. The prosecutors felt that in this way, race would not matter.

But that was not the case. Women overall were more likely to vote not guilty, with black women in particular being more likely to see Simpson as a victim.[9] These women had seen numerous examples of racism and injustice against the black community, including years of police brutality. It was easy for them to see Simpson as another black man being wronged by the criminal justice system.

Prosecutors accepted a mostly female jury. There were ten women and two men. Nine jurors were black, two were white, and one was Hispanic.[10]

### JURY FACTS

Jury selection was one of the most important aspects of pretrial preparations for Simpson's defense. As it turned out, they ended up with a jury that was very favorable to their side. Prospective jurors were asked to complete a long questionnaire. It covered a wide variety of questions, from whether they had ever experienced domestic violence to whether they were fans of USC Trojans football. Many of the responses were favorable to the defense. No one on the jury was a regular newspaper reader, but most watched TV news. Almost half had reported a negative interaction with police. And nine of them felt Simpson was less likely to be a murderer simply because he was a professional athlete.

## The Two Sides

Marcia Clark was chosen as the lead prosecutor. She had worked in the district attorney's

# THE SIMPSON JURY

**9** jurors were black; **2** were white; **1** was Hispanic

The 12-person jury in O. J. Simpson's murder trial was composed of mostly women and mostly people of color.

office for many years. She was known to be a passionate and aggressive prosecutor. This did not always sit well with juries. Clark cared deeply about her cases. But her style did not always earn her sympathy, as she was perceived by some jurors as confrontational and aggressive.

Clark's co-prosecutor was Christopher Darden. Darden had limited experience as a trial lawyer. But as a black man, he brought an important perspective to the prosecution beyond his legal expertise. Prosecutors strategized that Darden would be able to earn the trust of black jurors in a way that Clark would be unable to do.

On the other side, Simpson had assembled the best defense team that money could buy. They were dubbed the "Dream Team," and they were led by Robert Shapiro.[11] Shapiro had worked with many famous clients. He began the trial as Simpson's lead defense attorney. The team had other experienced attorneys including

## AFFORDING THE "DREAM TEAM"

Simpson got the best lawyers he could for his defense. Such defense comes at a price. Simpson's lawyers were estimated to cost him $50,000 a day. Even as an ex–football star, it was more than Simpson could afford. He made most of the money by selling sports memorabilia. Associates brought Simpson items to autograph in jail. They then sold those items to help pay for the case. This was one way Simpson's celebrity status helped him fight in the case.

Prosecutors Marcia Clark, *right*, and Christopher Darden speak in the courtroom.

F. Lee Bailey and Alan Dershowitz, and it utilized experts in DNA evidence, which was a new scientific field at that time.

Simpson's team also included Johnnie Cochran, who was one of the most famous defense attorneys in the country in 1994. A black man himself, he had represented several famous black clients such as singers Michael Jackson and James Brown. Cochran became well known for exposing police abuses of power, especially abuses against black people. Charming and persuasive, Cochran was very popular with juries.

On July 22, 1994, Simpson formally pleaded not guilty to the murders. Facing murder charges is a huge, daunting challenge. Most defendants—particularly impoverished people and many people of color—are unable to fight against the powerful resources available to state prosecutors. But Simpson was no ordinary defendant. With his money, fame, and ability to hire anyone, he was able to fight.

CHAPTER FIVE

# THE TRIAL BEGINS

Darden spoke the first words on behalf of the prosecution on January 24, 1995. In front of 12 jurors and millions of people watching at home, he laid out the prosecution's case. Darden argued that jurors may have thought they knew Simpson from seeing him on TV and in movies, but in reality, he was a violent abuser.

Darden painted a picture of Simpson's control over his wife. Simpson had known Brown since she was a teenager, barely out of high school. He provided everything for her. And when he got upset, he was violent with her.

The prosecution played Brown's 911 call from 1993. They cited this as evidence that Simpson had lost control of Brown. And without control, he got more violent. "It finally became clear that she wanted to live her own life," Darden said.

**Darden explains the prosecution's argument against Simpson.**

"[And] he was not going to be a part of it. . . . He could not accept that loss of control. And he wouldn't, and he didn't."[1]

## The Prosecution's Version

It was known that Simpson attended his daughter's dance recital on the night of the murders. Brown and her family were also there. The prosecution alleged that afterward, there was tension between Simpson, Brown, and Brown's family. The Browns had agreed to go to dinner at a nearby restaurant but made it clear Simpson was not invited. It was another example of Brown moving on without him, and it made him angry.

Simpson told his houseguest, Kato Kaelin, that he was upset about not being invited to dinner. The two of them went to McDonald's at approximately 9:10 p.m. The crucial events of June 12, 1994, happened

### TV DRAMA

Cameras in a courtroom were not new in 1994. The US Supreme Court had ruled that courts could use them back in 1981. In 1991, a channel devoted just to courtroom proceedings, Court TV, began airing. It was perfectly timed for the Simpson case. Instead of just broadcasting the trial, Court TV personalities presented analysis and commentary. It made for dramatic viewing. The case was also covered extensively by most major TV news networks, nearly from the moment of the murders. It made it hard for jurors to stay unbiased as so many people had heard about the crime before the trial and had watched the famous chase. Everyone was watching and talking about the case. The publicity could have influenced the verdict.

in the first 70 minutes after Kaelin and Simpson arrived home from McDonald's. That was the period in which Simpson could not explain his whereabouts.

The last person to see Simpson before the murders was Kaelin. Kaelin last saw Simpson when they returned from dinner at 9:35 p.m. Then at 10:40, he heard the thumps against the walls of the guesthouse. He saw Simpson again shortly after that, getting into the car that took him to the airport.

At approximately 9:37 p.m., Brown's mother realized she had left her glasses at the restaurant. She called her daughter. Brown then called the restaurant and talked to her friend

Ronald Goldman

Ronald Goldman, a server. He had just gotten off work and said he would bring the glasses to Brown to give to her mother later.

Prosecutors believed that the killings took place around 10:15 p.m. That was when neighbors heard Brown's Akita barking. Simpson, the prosecutors said, drove over to Brown's house intending to kill her. He knocked her unconscious and then stabbed her several times, they said. Goldman, on an errand to return the glasses, was merely in the wrong place at the wrong time.

Simpson then raced away from South Bundy Drive in the Bronco, the prosecution alleged. When the police went to the Rockingham estate to notify Simpson of Brown's death, they noticed that the Bronco looked as if it had been parked quickly in front of the house. It was sitting at an angle from the curb to the street.

## SOLD STORIES

There were two key witnesses the jury never heard from. This was because the witnesses sold their stories to news organizations. This made their stories questionable, as they might have been motivated only by money.

Jill Shively claimed to have seen Simpson fleeing from the area of South Bundy Drive in his Bronco the night of the murders. She said she knew it was Simpson because he almost crashed into her car. Shively sold her story to the TV news show *Hard Copy* for $5,000.

Jose Camacho was the employee who sold Simpson a kitchen knife six weeks before the murders. He sold his story to the *National Enquirer* newspaper for $12,500. But tests later proved that knife was not the murder weapon.

## A Trail of Blood

At some point, Simpson cut his hand. He also lost one of the gloves he was wearing, the prosecution alleged. They said that led to a trail of blood that was hard to ignore. Blood droplets led from Brown's condo to Simpson's Bronco, then up the driveway at Rockingham, and even into Simpson's bedroom.

And it was not just Simpson's blood. Blood from both Brown and Goldman was found away from the crime scene. It was on the glove found at the Simpson property. And there was not only blood from Brown and Goldman on the glove but also some of their hair, fibers matching the shirt Goldman was wearing, and fibers from the Bronco carpet.

Simpson's blood was found inside the Bronco, and so was Brown's and Goldman's. Brown's blood was found on a sock of Simpson's in his bedroom. For the prosecution, it was clear as day. "That trail of blood from Bundy through his own Ford Bronco and into his house in Rockingham is devastating proof of his guilt," Clark told the jury.[2]

## Other Evidence, but No Murder Weapon

Clark and the prosecution felt the blood evidence was enough on its own. But there was much more that tied Simpson to the crime. There was also a ski mask found at the scene. Fibers found inside the mask matched the carpet in Simpson's Bronco.

There were also hairs that matched Simpson's hair. Simpson's hairs were also found on Goldman's shirt.

Shoe prints were found in the blood. Police never found an actual shoe that Simpson wore to match to the prints. But investigators suspected the prints belonged to Simpson because they were size 12 (Simpson's size), and they came from a rare, expensive type of shoe. The shoes were made by Italian shoemaker Bruno Magli and cost hundreds of dollars. Only 200 pairs of the shoes were shipped to the United States.[3] The store Bloomingdale's, where Simpson often shopped, was one of five

Police found large amounts of blood on the sidewalk and street outside Brown's home.

stores that carried them. Simpson, however, claimed the shoes were ugly and said he would never buy them.

The evidence piled up. But what the prosecution did not have was the knife used as the murder weapon. It was not for a lack of searching. Investigators looked for days in and around the Chicago hotel where Simpson stayed the night of the murders. They even used a satellite that could detect metal objects from space. But the knife was never found.

Prosecutors discovered that Simpson had bought a long kitchen knife just a month before the murders. But the knife was found in the Simpson home and was in brand-new condition. It was never introduced as evidence.

## Relying on DNA

The prosecution did not have the murder weapon. They did not have anyone who saw the murders happen. The matching blood from the crime scene and the Simpson property was vital to the case. But to make their case stronger, the prosecution had a new field of science to help. Deoxyribonucleic acid, commonly known as DNA, is a genetic marker for each person. It is present in human cells, which are present in blood.

Scientists can test a DNA sample to figure out which person it may have come from. DNA was a relatively new science at the time of the Simpson trial. It helped the prosecution tie Simpson to the crime scene. Blood samples in both places

## ABOUT DNA

DNA is found in every cell in the human body. That's anywhere from 50 trillion to 100 trillion cells.[4] So it is often easy to find DNA that a person has left behind. But matching that to a specific person is much more difficult. Most DNA looks similar from person to person. Scientists look for the similarities between two DNA samples to try and make a match. Scientists are generally looking for an exact match between samples, but even a partial match can be useful. A partial match can exclude a lot of people from being considered the source of the DNA sample in question, such as a sample left behind at a crime scene. In this way, DNA evidence can help prove someone committed a crime, or it can free someone wrongly accused. Reexamining DNA evidence found at a crime scene can rule out someone accused if the DNA evidence does not match the suspect's DNA markers.

were tested for certain genetic markers. DNA evidence could show it was highly likely the samples matched. But the jurors were unfamiliar with this science which may have made them feel uncomfortable.

Clark was tasked with having to explain this new science to the jury. It is a complex science, not as simple as saying, "This blood came from this man." DNA evidence can accurately narrow down a list of potential suspects, but it isn't specific enough to point to one person. This complexity was another hurdle that the prosecution had to overcome.

## Defense Responses

Simpson's legal team sought to refute all of the evidence that the prosecution presented. Their argument had several things going for it. Nobody could place Simpson at the crime scene.

There were none of Simpson's fingerprints at the crime scene. Everything could be explained as a coincidence.

The shoe prints? Anyone could have bought those shoes. Hairs found at the scene? Those weren't subject to DNA testing; they were only examined under a microscope. They could have come from any black person, the defense argued. The cut on Simpson's hand? Simpson had already said that happened in Chicago. All the defense had to do was make the jury question the evidence.

The hardest thing for the defense to explain was the DNA-tested blood evidence. So the defense alleged that the evidence simply didn't exist. Playing off of the newness and unfamiliarity of DNA science, the defense argued that the blood evidence was all created just to make Simpson look guilty.

## CONSPIRACY THEORIES

Despite the evidence publicly presented during Simpson's trial, people across the country developed many other theories about the murders. These theorists were likely encouraged by the celebrity aspect of the case. One conspiracy theory involved Simpson's son Jason. The theory was that he was the real killer and that the only reason Simpson was on the scene was to protect his son. One of the more bizarre conspiracy theories was that Simpson was under mind-control hypnosis to carry out the murders. According to this theory, the crime was then going to be used to start a race war in the United States.

CHAPTER SIX

# THE GLOVE DOESN'T FIT

The Simpson defense team was faced with a mountain of evidence. None of it proved Simpson was guilty. But they had no piece of evidence to prove Simpson was not guilty. The defense had to work on reducing the impact of the evidence presented by the prosecution. Every piece of evidence that they could eliminate would increase the doubt in the minds of the jurors.

There was more evidence that the jury never got to hear. Four days before the murders, Nicole Brown had called a women's shelter. She said that Simpson was stalking her and that she feared for her life. The prosecution decided not to submit this as evidence. The call was not recorded and was just based on a shelter worker's memory. The prosecutors felt that Judge Lance Ito would dismiss it as hearsay, a type of secondhand statement that can't be proven.

**Simpson, *bottom right*, speaks with his "Dream Team" of defense lawyers.**

Also dismissed as hearsay was something Simpson supposedly told his friend Rosey Grier, another ex-NFL player. Grier regularly visited Simpson in jail. Once while they were meeting, a police officer overheard Simpson say, "I didn't mean to do it."[1] Grier then reportedly encouraged Simpson to confess. Ito ruled that this could not be admitted as evidence.

Other evidence not presented to the jury included the cash, disguises, and passport found in the Bronco after the police chase. All this evidence could have been influential. But the prosecutors thought it could be interpreted as Simpson just being distraught over the loss of his ex-wife, so they did not show it to the jury.

### FROGMEN

Simpson's acting career had an eerie overlap with real life in 1994. A few months before the murders, Simpson filmed an episode of a new TV show called *Frogmen*. He starred as the leader of a team of Navy SEALs. In one scene, Simpson's character holds a knife to a woman's throat. The prosecution decided not to show the video to the jury. The episode never aired, and no copies circulated among the public. It was Simpson's last acting role.

## Denying DNA

When DNA samples are collected, it is important that investigators follow certain procedures. The samples must be properly sealed in sterile containers. Any outside substance can alter a DNA sample. Records must be kept. Investigators have to know when the sample was taken, who delivered it to the lab, and when.

A key part of the defense involved exposing errors in how the DNA samples had been handled by police. Blood samples went missing. People had access to the samples when they should not have. Witnesses for the prosecution admitted to these kinds of errors.

In one example, 1.5 milliliters of Simpson's blood went missing. The prosecution could not refute this, as the police did not keep proper records of how much blood was taken in the first place. The blood that was taken did not even make it to the lab right away. It took several hours to arrive, leading to questions about what had happened to the missing blood.

The DNA evidence was also poorly understood by the jury. The Simpson defense brought in Barry Scheck, an expert in the field of DNA. He was able to minimize the DNA evidence, which was central to the prosecution's case against Simpson. Scheck attacked the testing methods and the conclusions investigators drew from them.

**In 1992, Barry Scheck cofounded The Innocence Project, a nonprofit organization dedicated to using DNA evidence to free falsely accused people from prison.**

The DNA evidence could have been

## JURY PROTEST

Starting in January, the Simpson jury was isolated from the public because of the famous nature of the trial, a process called sequestration. As the trial dragged on for weeks and months, tensions rose between the jury and Judge Lance Ito, and among the jurors themselves. At one point, thirteen jurors (including alternates) staged a protest. Four jurors walked into court one day wearing black.

The jury tensions created the possibility of a mistrial. Many jurors had already been dismissed for violations such as lying on their questionnaires and selling their stories to write books. Ito tried to keep the jury happy throughout the long trial. He arranged trips to sporting events and even to a taping of *The Tonight Show*. Only four original jurors remained by the end of the trial.

overwhelming. A scientist testifying for the prosecution said the chance that the blood came from anyone but Simpson was one in 170 million. The scientist said the chance that the blood on the sock came from anyone but Nicole Brown was one in 21 billion.[2] But the prosecution failed to make these statistics clear to the jury.

## Attacking the Police

Besides the mishandling of DNA evidence, the defense also cited sloppy police work. In one instance, police used a blanket from inside Brown's home to cover her body. With no knowledge of whose DNA was on the blanket, it could have crucially contaminated the crime scene.

There also was a bloody thumbprint found on the gate to the Brown home. Detective Mark Fuhrman, one of the first LAPD officers on the scene, documented it in his notes.

But what happened to the print is a mystery. Either it was taken into evidence but never logged, or it was cleaned up before being examined.

Investigators also left their own bloody shoe prints all over the crime scene. There were more of them than from the killer. All of these lapses in procedure reduced the credibility of the investigation.

A detective investigates the murder scene. Simpson's lawyers argued the crime scene was not properly handled by police.

But the defense also alleged more than shoddy police work. They alleged that police may have intentionally tried to frame Simpson by planting evidence. According to the defense, this explained the lack of record keeping. It was more than just making mistakes—it was to hide a police conspiracy, they said.

One of the defense's arguments that supported planted evidence was the presence of EDTA in some of the blood evidence. EDTA is a substance added to blood samples in a lab that keeps the sample from breaking down. To the defense, this meant the blood was taken from the lab and planted at the crime scene. But all blood has EDTA in it. Some is natural, and some is artificial. There was no way to tell the difference at the time.

The defense knew the jury would be well aware of L.A.'s history with racism. Jurors certainly remembered the Rodney King case. This was the basis of the defense's strategy of portraying the LAPD as untrustworthy in this case.

## The Fuhrman Tapes

The defense made Detective Fuhrman the face of the police conspiracy. He was the one who discovered a key piece of evidence: the bloody glove behind Kaelin's guesthouse. But the defense argued he did not discover the glove at all. They said he was the one who put it there.

The gloves were a gift from Brown to Simpson in 1990. The left one was found at the crime scene. The right one was on the Simpson property. It was soaked in blood that DNA testing indicated came from both victims and Simpson. A strand of hair that appeared to match Brown's was also on the glove.

Fuhrman testified twice during the trial. The first time, the defense tried to paint Fuhrman as a racist. They asked if he ever used racial slurs. Fuhrman denied ever doing so. But videotapes soon surfaced of Fuhrman using the slurs years earlier. When called to the stand later in the trial, Fuhrman was asked if he had lied in police reports or planted any evidence. He used his constitutional right to not answer any questions.

It was a big win for the defense. One of the case's investigators was a proven liar and racist. The prosecution admitted that Fuhrman was racist, but they argued that should play no part in whether Simpson was found guilty.

### FIXING THE SCENE

Toward the end of the trial, the jury was taken to inspect Brown's home and Simpson's estate, which were no longer active crime scenes at the time of the trial. The defense took measures to present a more favorable image to the jury. In Simpson's house, they took down the numerous photos of Simpson with white friends and replaced them with ones featuring more black people so that Simpson might appear as more of a sympathetic figure for the largely black jury. Simpson also owned some pieces of art with nude models; these were replaced with ones that were deemed more family friendly.

# THE GLOVES

Showing whether the gloves fit was one way to demonstrate whether the gloves were Simpson's. But even though the gloves did not fit in court, there were other signs pointing to them being Simpson's. The prosecution produced a photo from an NFL game in 1991 when Simpson was working as a broadcaster. In the photo, he was wearing dark brown leather gloves on the sideline. To identify the gloves for certain, the prosecution called an executive from the manufacturer to the stand. The gloves were only sold at the Bloomingdale's department store. Simpson and his wife shopped at Bloomingdale's, and a saleswoman testified to having sold Brown a pair of the gloves in 1990.

**The famous bloody gloves now reside with all the other evidence from the Simpson case at the Los Angeles County District Attorney's office, just in case they're ever needed for a new trial.**

## Trying On the Glove

Prosecutor Christopher Darden had an idea: make Simpson try on the gloves. He believed that seeing Simpson wearing the gloves would make a statement to the jury that they could not ignore. Marcia Clark and the rest of the prosecution team were nervous about it.

The gloves had been soaked in blood. Leather tends to contract when wet, and the gloves could have shrunk once dry. The gloves had also been frozen and thawed several times in evidence. Plus, Simpson would have to wear surgical gloves underneath the leather gloves as he tried them on. But Darden had him go through with it anyway.

It became a defining scene from the case. Simpson put a glove on his left hand. He pulled and tugged at it to try and get it past his knuckles. He even held his hand up to show the jury how he could barely get it on. Then he did the same with the right glove. They appeared not to go on past his wrists.

This was a huge embarrassment for the prosecution, and it was a victory for the defense. It was the basis of one of the most famous quotes of the trial, from Defense Attorney Johnnie Cochran. "If it doesn't fit, you must acquit," Cochran told the jury, referring to the gloves.[3]

In court, Simpson struggles to put on a glove found at the crime scene.

CHAPTER SEVEN

# THE VERDICT

The Fuhrman testimony was one of the last major moments in the trial. It took place on September 6, 1995. On September 22, the defense and prosecution rested their cases. The jury began its deliberations on October 2.

It was one of the longest high-profile murder trials of the 1990s. The jury was sequestered for 265 days, which was an all-time record nationwide.[1] Once the jury went into deliberation, the world waited. But people did not have to wait long. The jury reached a verdict in only four hours.

Many experts thought the verdict would take days or weeks. So when the speedy verdict was ready, neither the defense nor the prosecution were still at the courthouse. Ito ruled that the verdict was to be sealed and announced the next morning.

**Some fans continued to support Simpson throughout the trial, even leaving signs at his house.**

WE ♥
O.J. YA
FIGHT ON!!
WE SUPPORT
YOU O.J!
#32 FOREVER!

## The Anticipation Builds

Much like the Bronco police chase, the verdict announcement was broadcast live around the world. Estimates vary, but between 95 million and 150 million people tuned in to watch. Only approximately 94 million people tuned in to the Super Bowl the following January.[2]

As the verdict was read on TV, trading slowed on the New York Stock Exchange. Long-distance phone calls were reduced by 58 percent.[3] Water usage decreased as people avoided going to the bathroom. All eyes were on the Los Angeles County Courthouse. Even President Bill Clinton left the Oval Office to watch the verdict on TV with his staff.

The city of Los Angeles took security measures in case of violence. Whatever the verdict was, the city did not want a

People across the country watched the Simpson verdict read on TV.

repeat of the civil unrest that followed the Rodney King beating verdicts. The LAPD staffed extra officers and placed officers on horseback around the courthouse. Like everyone else waiting for the verdict, they did not know what the reaction would be.

It was just after 10:00 a.m. The trial of O. J. Simpson had been going on for 474 days. There had been 99 days of testimony in which 72 witnesses were called.[4] It would all finally be over in just a matter of minutes.

## "We the Jury . . ."

The families of both victims were at the courthouse. Judge Ito gave a warning before the verdict was read that any outbursts would result in ejection from the courtroom. The head juror reviewed the verdict to make sure it matched what the jury had decided the day before. Once she confirmed it, she gave the verdict to court clerk Deidre Robinson to read for the court.

Simpson and his defense team were asked to stand and face the jury. Simpson sighed as Robinson began to read.

"We the jury in the above-entitled action find the defendant, Orenthal James Simpson, not guilty of the crime of murder," Robinson said.[5]

Simpson closed his lips tightly, then weakly smiled and whispered, "Thank you."[6] Cochran pumped his fist and then patted Simpson on the back. Robinson continued to read the verdict, confirming Simpson was not guilty of the murders.

As Simpson said thank you toward the jury, two jurors smiled back at him. Another gave a raised fist, a symbol of support for the Black Power movement. But as Simpson celebrated, cries were heard from the audience.

## Devastation

Fred Goldman, Ronald Goldman's father, had been a steady presence during the trial. He was an outspoken advocate for his son's memory. And he was certain beyond a shadow of a doubt that Simpson had murdered him.

When the verdict was read, Goldman clutched his wife and his daughter, Kim, Ron's sister. Kim Goldman sobbed as the jury's not guilty verdict was broadcast to the world. "Murderer,"

Defense attorney Johnnie Cochran, *right*, hugs Simpson after the verdict is read.

was all Fred Goldman would say, whispering it under his breath. He repeated it later in front of cameras upon leaving the courtroom. He called his son's murder the "worst nightmare" of his life. "[But] this was the second," he said, referring to the verdict.[7]

### DARDEN'S REGRET

It was Christopher Darden's decision to have Simpson try on the bloody gloves. Many people blamed him for losing the case right in that moment. But reflecting on the case in 2016, Darden expressed no regrets over that decision. He believed that the case had already been lost by that point in the trial. Having Simpson try on the gloves was merely a desperate move to try to change the course of the case. However, Darden did have one regret. He said he wished he had never joined the case in the first place.

As for Clark and Darden, the gravity of what had just happened hit them right away. As the jurors were polled to confirm their not guilty votes, Darden stared at the jurors. None of them looked back. Clark did not look at the jury.

## Celebration

It was a different story for the Simpson family. Simpson's sister said she felt like dancing. His mother reiterated that they always believed her son was innocent. Simpson's son Jason read a statement on behalf of his father, who did not attend a posttrial press conference for security reasons.

"I am relieved that this part of the incredible nightmare that occurred on June 12, 1994, is over with," Simpson's statement said.[8] Simpson went on to say that his number one goal in life going forward would be to track down his ex-wife's real killer. He believed that in time, evidence would come to light that he could not have been the murderer.

Within about an hour after the verdict was read, Simpson was back at home on Rockingham Avenue. It was a fitting scene as the whole ordeal seemed to come full circle. Al Cowlings drove Simpson home, just as he had driven him in the white Bronco on June 17, 1994. When they parked, they hugged and celebrated. It was the same driveway where the LAPD had arrested them after the chase.

**Darden was fired from his job at the district attorney's after losing the Simpson case. He later became a law professor and legal commentator.**

Also like after the chase, there were supporters gathered outside the home. They chanted, "O. J.! O. J.!"[9] Simpson and his friends and family celebrated with a party in the house that lasted long into the night. There was even a saxophone player on hand.

But not everyone gathered on Rockingham was there to support Simpson. One observer, Shane Novak, pointed out how it could be seen as disrespectful to have a party when two murders were still unsolved. "What about Ron Goldman?"

Novak said. "There's no one playing a saxophone at Ron Goldman's party now."[10]

## ROBERT SHAPIRO

Defense Attorney Robert Shapiro rarely spoke about the case for decades afterward. But reflecting on it in 2016, he declined to say whether he thought Simpson was guilty or innocent. He also said he knew that Simpson would not be able to put the gloves on, as they did not fit Shapiro either and Simpson's hands were much bigger. "If you look at it from a moral point of view a lot of people would say, 'He absolutely did it,'" Shapiro said. "I deal in legal justice."[12] Shapiro acknowledged the legal system is often not fair.

## Making Sense of the Verdict

Once the trial ended, the jury was free to discuss the case. Many chose to do so. And in general, they felt satisfied with how they voted. But few of them felt that way because they believed Simpson was innocent.

Juror Anise Aschenbach actually believed Simpson was guilty. But a juror's responsibility is to decide guilt or innocence beyond a reasonable doubt. Aschenbach, and several other jurors, felt that the prosecution did not meet that standard.

Jurors mentioned the numerous missteps the prosecution made with evidence. They said the DNA samples had been mishandled. They mentioned the questionable police work. Juror Lionel Cryer put it bluntly. "It was garbage in, garbage out," he said of the evidence.[11]

Race certainly played a factor in the trial. But jurors disagreed on how big of a factor it was. It was a major factor for Aschenbach. She said it was how the defense portrayed Detective Fuhrman as a racist that opened the possibility Simpson was framed. Some other jurors dismissed race as a primary factor.

Nevertheless, it was impossible to separate race from the verdict. In a poll of the general public, opinions seemed split down racial lines. A poll taken just after the verdict showed 47 percent of people felt the verdict was right, and 44 percent felt it was wrong. Nine percent had no opinion. But just 42 percent of white voters agreed with the verdict, compared with 78 percent of black voters.[13]

### GLEN ROGERS

Approximately one month after the verdict, serial killer Glen Rogers was arrested. He boasted of killing more than 70 women, including Nicole Brown Simpson. No evidence connects Rogers with the crime. But Rogers claimed he was hired by Simpson to steal back some diamond earrings from Brown's home. When Goldman unexpectedly arrived, he said, he was forced to kill both of them. The LAPD investigated the claims but believed it was more of an attempt by Rogers to be tried in California, where it was less likely he would receive the death penalty. The murders of Brown and Goldman did not resemble the rest of Rogers's crimes.

## Trial of the Century

Whether the verdict was right or wrong, there was no doubt the impact of the trial was massive. Even while it was still going on, it came to be called the "Trial of the Century."[14] Its celebrity defendant, the brutal nature of the crime, and the public way it played out with the Bronco chase drew worldwide attention.

## MOVIES ABOUT THE CASE

As if the trial wasn't must-see TV itself, the first movie made about the crime came out before the trial was even over. The Fox network aired the TV movie *The OJ Simpson Story* on January 31, 1995. The movie's production started even before the Bronco chase happened. It was originally set to debut in September, but was pushed back after concerns it could affect the jury. Since that first movie, the Simpson case has been featured in several movies, documentaries, and TV shows.

In a time before smartphones, people were glued to whatever news coverage they could get. That meant following the newspaper and TV coverage of the trial, which was a relatively new concept. Before the spread of memes entered popular culture, phrases like "If it doesn't fit, you must acquit" circulated among the public.

The trial in many cases took precedence over significant world events. US involvement in a war in Bosnia plus the bombing of a federal building in Oklahoma City took place in 1995. But those took a back seat in public memory to the Simpson trial. And interest in the case was not about to go away anytime soon.

## CHAPTER EIGHT

# THE LAWSUIT

Simpson may have been free in the months after the verdict. But the life he went back to was anything but normal. Simpson had been a beloved public figure. Instead of resuming that celebrity life after the trial, Simpson saw much of the world treating him like a murderer. Many people who had followed the trial had come to their own conclusion that Simpson was actually guilty.

Simpson lost out on acting jobs. He was kicked out of his country club. His agent dropped him as a client. People even put up signs in Brentwood. One said, "Welcome to Brentwood. Home of the Brentwood Butcher."[1] But to the Brown and Goldman families, these were small consequences. Their loved ones were still dead, and they believed Simpson had done it. They felt that Simpson simply losing some luxuries was not a fitting punishment. He could not be tried again for the same crime, but there was another legal way for the Brown and

**Simpson arrives at a meeting related to the civil lawsuit filed against him after he was found not guilty.**

Goldman families to hold Simpson accountable for what they believed he had done.

## The Civil Trial

In 1996, the Goldman and Brown families sued Simpson. A lawsuit is a civil action, very different from a criminal case like the one that saw Simpson not guilty of murder. The civil suit was for wrongful death, meaning it claimed that Simpson's actions caused the deaths of Brown and Goldman. If the jury for the civil case decided it was more likely than not that Simpson did commit the murders, he would be forced to pay damages in the form of money.

Not only was the legal structure different; the proceedings were dramatically different, too. The rules set by the judge in the civil case, Hiroshi Fujisaki, were different from those in the criminal

### WHAT IS A CIVIL CASE?

The main difference between a civil case and a criminal case is that a civil case is a dispute between two people or organizations. A criminal case always involves the government looking to prosecute someone suspected of breaking a law. A common type of civil case is a lawsuit in which someone has lost money because of the actions of another person. Wrongful death is the way civil courts address murder. In civil cases, there is no jail time as punishment. The defendant in a wrongful death lawsuit can be found liable for the deaths and made to compensate for that liability with money.

case. Fujisaki did not allow any cameras in the courtroom. Lawyers were prohibited from talking to the media.

There were also no allegations of racism. The court decided that introducing such evidence was pure speculation and that the jury should not base its decision on such remarks. And because the civil case was tried in Santa Monica, the jury pool was far different than the one in the criminal case. The civil case jury was mostly white.

Also, Simpson took the stand in his defense. He declined to do so during the criminal trial. For the first time, Simpson had to directly confront the evidence in front of an audience. What about the gloves? What about the domestic violence? For four hours, Simpson answered these questions. He denied he ever hit Brown. He again and again asserted his innocence.

Jurors in the civil trial heard much of the same evidence that was presented in the criminal case. They knew all about the history of domestic abuse, the bloody gloves, and the extensive blood evidence.

They also heard about the bloody shoe prints that matched Simpson's size-12 feet. But in the criminal case, the size of the shoe could be dismissed as a coincidence. They could have been anyone's shoes. One of the new pieces of evidence in the civil case was a photo of Simpson wearing the exact model of shoe years earlier.

Simpson had been photographed on the sidelines of an NFL game while working as a broadcaster. The photo was taken in Buffalo, New York, in 1993. The photographer, E. J. Flammer, discovered the photo in a box in December 1996.

The photo itself didn't prove anything. But with Simpson's earlier statement that he would never wear such shoes, the photo appeared to show he was trying to hide something. The photo was a major development in the civil case.

The trial began in October 1996 and continued until February 1997. On February 4, the jury reached a verdict. Simpson was found to be liable for the deaths of Nicole Brown and Ronald Goldman.

As punishment, Simpson was ordered to pay the victims' families a total of $33.5 million. It was a massive amount of money. In similar civil trials, the award is typically around two percent of the defendant's net worth. At his peak, Simpson was worth $10 million. But after paying for his very expensive legal defense, that number had dwindled.

In court, Simpson argued that he didn't have the money to pay. He claimed he was in debt $850,000. But the decision was based on his earning potential. And some legal experts, such as law professor Robert Rabin, believed the high dollar-amount was a message. It said that Simpson may have gotten away with murder, but the world should know what really happened.

The victims' families were thrilled. While it in no way made up for the loss of their loved ones, it was a small bit of consequence for Simpson. Collecting the money would be another matter, however. Simpson was never going to have $33.5 million.

## Curious Behavior

Despite his promise to hunt for the "real killer," Simpson spent the rest of the 1990s and the early 2000s largely promoting himself.[2] He remained in the public eye and did not shy away from discussing the case. In fact, it became his primary point of notability. He was no longer O. J. Simpson, Hall of Fame football player. He was O. J. Simpson, possible murderer.

Simpson always asserted his innocence. He felt it was unfair that the public continued to blame him for the murders. But his

Patti Goldman, *left*, and her husband, Fred Goldman, visit Ronald Goldman's grave.

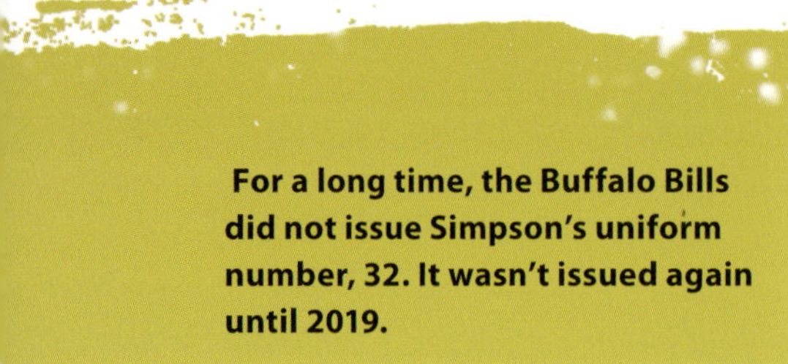
For a long time, the Buffalo Bills did not issue Simpson's uniform number, 32. It wasn't issued again until 2019.

behavior did not reduce the suspicions of many that he was guilty of the crimes.

In an interview with *Esquire* magazine in 1998, Simpson compared himself to Jesus in how much persecution he had faced. He also felt the civil judgment against him was totally unfair. And he made a famous comment that many took as a kind of veiled confession. "Let's say I committed this crime," Simpson said. "Even if I did do this, it would have to have been because I loved her very much, right?"[3]

Months later, Simpson did a television interview with British talk show host Ruby Wax. In one segment, Simpson pretended to stab Wax with a banana. It seemed odd that anyone would joke about being accused of a double murder. Simpson's

## THE SIMPSON CHILDREN

Simpson's children stood by him through the criminal trial and beyond. His two oldest children come from his first marriage to Marguerite Whitley. Arnelle is the oldest and lives in Florida. Two years younger is Jason, who lives in Atlanta. Simpson's younger children, from his marriage to Brown, are Sydney and Justin. Sydney graduated from Boston University in 2010 and lives in Florida. Justin also lives in Florida and is a realtor. Sydney and Justin were very young at the time of the murders; they were sleeping at their mother's house while she was killed. As the older siblings, Arnelle and Jason publicly spoke out defending their father throughout the trial.

increasingly erratic behavior left him fewer and fewer defenders.

With his acting and promotion work drying up, the primary way for Simpson to generate an income was by capitalizing on his waning football fame. He routinely signed autographs and auctioned off merchandise to make whatever money he could.

## GOODBYE ROCKINGHAM

Simpson was evicted from his home on Rockingham Avenue in 1997 after failing to pay the mortgage. A new owner purchased the house for $4 million, but given the home's notorious past and the fact that it had fallen into disrepair, he opted to demolish the house and build a new one. "It's not my house, and I could care less," Simpson said at the time.[4] A new house was later built on the same site, and no part of the Simpson estate remains.

In 1999, a group of protesters paid $16,000 at an auction for various items of Simpson's football memorabilia. They took the items to the Los Angeles County courthouse, where Simpson had been found not guilty in 1995, and set them ablaze. The burning was to protest failures in the criminal justice system, not only in Simpson's case, but in general.

There was still some interest in Simpson's football career, though. At the same auction, Simpson's Heisman Trophy sold for $255,500. It was the first time in history a Heisman Trophy had been sold.

CHAPTER NINE

# SIMPSON GOES TO PRISON

In November 2006, Simpson made his boldest statement yet about the murders. It came in the form of a book. But it wasn't just a simple memoir or autobiography. Simpson's book, entitled *If I Did It*, was a hypothetical description of how the murders would have been committed had Simpson been the one responsible.

Though Simpson was listed as the author, he did not write the book. In a strange twist of fate, the actual author was Pablo Fenjves, Brown's neighbor and the witness who heard her dog wailing on the night of the killings. Simpson claimed he had nothing to do with the book, while Fenjves claimed that he and Simpson collaborated.

Simpson was to be paid $600,000 to say he had written the book. He also was to give a televised interview. News of

**A promotional cover of the book *If I Did It***

IF I DID IT

the book's release generated controversy right away. Judith Regan, the book's publisher, who would be conducting the TV interview, defended her involvement with the book. "This is a historic case, and I consider this his confession," she said.[1]

## If I Did It

The book first describes Simpson's marriage to Brown. It acknowledges the violence that took place but insists that it was always Brown who was the instigator. Further, the book alleges that Brown had criminal ties through her group of friends, including drug dealers.

The hypothetical description of the crime is contained to only one chapter of the book. That chapter first describes the events earlier in the evening. Simpson attended his daughter's dance recital and then returned home, later going out for dinner with Kaelin. It is at that point that the book introduces an accomplice, identified only as "Charlie."[2]

According to the book's hypothetical scenario, Charlie told Simpson that Brown had been drinking and doing drugs. Simpson concluded that he should scare Brown, and he and Charlie decided to drive over to South Bundy Drive. Simpson grabbed a wool hat, leather gloves, and a knife. Charlie held onto the knife to prevent Simpson from doing something rash.

Upon arriving at Brown's condo, the book states, the pair noted candles burning in the windows and presumed Brown was expecting company. Goldman arrived a short time later with Brown's mother's glasses. Simpson flew into a jealous rage and got into a screaming match with Brown, according to the book. As Goldman attempted to attack Simpson, Simpson grabbed the knife away from Charlie.

The book states that Simpson did not remember what happened next. It says he just remembered waking up totally covered in blood. Then he bound up his clothes and gave them to Charlie along with the knife, telling him to take care of them.

According to the book, Simpson returned home after the killing. He snuck into the house to avoid the limo driver waiting for him, changed into clean clothes, and returned to the limo, the books states. He then flew to Chicago, where he was informed of his wife's death.

Simpson described his police interview and the Bronco chase in the rest of the book. It contained little new information, but he did fill in some details on the chase. Simpson wrote that he was trying to visit

## MARCIA CLARK

Saying that the Simpson trial "ruined my life," prosecutor Marcia Clark stopped practicing law entirely after the trial ended.[3] It was not just the verdict that bothered her. As a result of the famous trial, Clark became the victim of attacks on everything from her looks to her voice. Clark wrote a book about her experience in 1997, and it became a number one best seller. She then began writing fiction, penning two popular mystery series. She also created a TV legal drama called *The Fix* that aired on ABC in 2019.

Brown's grave on that day, but the LAPD had officers guarding it. Simpson also said he planned to kill himself but changed his mind and asked Cowlings to drive him home instead.

The details of the book's contents only leaked out through the media. That was because the book's publisher announced the project was canceled just weeks after it was announced. Rupert Murdoch, president of News Corporation, the publisher's parent company, called the book an "ill-conceived project" and apologized to the families of the victims.[4]

The Brown and Goldman families were outraged about the book as soon as it was announced. In the wake of its cancellation, however, they saw an opportunity not only to punish Simpson but also to collect at least some of the $33.5 million owed to them. Simpson had paid hardly any of the money up to that point.

The Goldman family was awarded the rights to the book in 2007. They arranged to publish it under the new title *If I Did It: Confessions of the Killer*. The book's cover design had the words *I Did It* in big red letters with the word *If* in tiny white type. The family also added its own commentary to the book.

## The Robbery

Simpson had well-documented money problems in the decades after his legal victory. Almost all of his income came from his NFL pension—which by law could not be taken as part of his civil trial payment owed to the Browns and Goldmans. Simpson also made money from memorabilia sales.

On September 13, 2007, Simpson recruited some fellow guests at a wedding he was attending in Las Vegas. He needed help retrieving some memorabilia that he claimed had been stolen from him. Simpson claimed Mike Gilbert, his former agent, stole the items from him. Gilbert had arranged for Simpson to autograph memorabilia from jail during the murder trial.

Simpson signs autographs in 2005. As it was difficult for him to find work after his murder trial, Simpson mostly made money selling memorabilia of himself.

How the items got to the Palace Station Hotel in Las Vegas wasn't clear. But Simpson wanted them back. And he planned to get them by any means necessary. A different memorabilia dealer had tipped off Simpson that the items were in Las Vegas.

Simpson and five men went over to the Palace Station. At least two of them were armed with guns, but Simpson was not. Once they arrived, Simpson took over. He ordered his men to keep everyone from leaving. Simpson confronted the two memorabilia dealers. One of them confirmed that he had bought some of the items from Gilbert.

The whole encounter lasted approximately six minutes. Simpson and his associates then loaded Simpson's memorabilia into their cars and took off. Among the items were pieces from Simpson's football career as well as artifacts from the trial, such as some of the ties Simpson wore in court.

### JUICED

Simpson had a short-lived reality TV series in 2006 called *Juiced*. It was a hidden-camera show in which Simpson would try to prank unsuspecting people. In one sketch, Simpson played a used car salesman trying to sell customers a white Ford Bronco. Then at the end, to surprise the guests with the fact that they had just been on a hidden-camera show, Simpson would shout out the catchphrase, "You've been juiced!"[5] The show was hugely controversial and only lasted for one pay-per-view special.

## Another Conviction

After Simpson and his crew left, one of the memorabilia dealers called the police. He told them he had just been robbed by O. J. Simpson. Simpson and many of his accomplices were arrested days later. For his part, Simpson claimed that no robbery took place. He alleged that all the items belonged to him, and he was merely taking them back. One of the memorabilia dealers admitted that during the encounter, Simpson directed his associates to take only items that belonged to him and leave everything else.

Simpson was charged with 12 different crimes, including assault with a deadly weapon and robbery. He faced significant prison time. Armed robbery alone could carry a sentence of 30 years. Simpson's lawyers argued their case that it was not a robbery. They argued Simpson didn't ask anyone to bring a gun. Instead, the lawyers argued, Simpson was just a victim of falling in with the wrong crowd and also of being targeted by police because of his famous past.

On October 3, 2008—13 years to the day after being found not guilty of the murders—Simpson was convicted on all 12 counts. He was sentenced to at least nine years in prison, with a maximum of 33. The 61-year-old Simpson would not get out of jail until he was 70 at the earliest.

## The Legacy

The passage of time, and Simpson serving time behind bars, did little to dim public interest in the saga. In 2016, a TV miniseries

A handcuffed Simpson speaks in court in 2008.

about the trial received rave reviews on the FX network. *The People vs. O.J. Simpson: American Crime Story* starred Cuba Gooding Jr. in the title role.

The series did more than just recount the events of the case. It also examined the case's impact on modern society: the worship of celebrity, struggling with race relations, and failures of the criminal justice system. In many ways, the Simpson case became more relevant with time.

## NO TV FOR O. J.

Even as a miniseries was airing that dramatized his life, Simpson wasn't able to watch it. While serving time at the Lovelock Correction Institution in Nevada, Simpson was unable to watch *The People vs. O.J. Simpson* because the prison did not have cable TV. But that did not stop Simpson from having opinions about it. He overheard details of the show from guards and felt the show portrayed his life inaccurately. He also thought lead actor Cuba Gooding Jr. was too short to play him.

**Simpson joined the social media site Twitter in June 2019. By the end of July, he had nearly 900,000 followers.**

Also in 2016, ESPN aired a five-part, 7.5-hour documentary called *O.J.: Made in America*. The documentary also broke down more of the thematic elements of the case, discussing in great detail its racial undercurrents. The documentary won an Academy Award the next year.

As for Simpson himself, he was released from prison in 2017 after serving the minimum nine years. By all accounts, he was a model prisoner and had few issues in being granted parole. Even one of the victims of the robbery testified at his hearing to say that Simpson would pose no threat to anyone.

After being released from prison, Simpson planned to move in with his daughter in Florida. But ultimately, he decided to stay in Las Vegas. Simpson continues to draw his NFL pension, which is estimated to be as much as $25,000 a month. He still owes the Brown and Goldman families a large amount of money from his civil trial, an amount that has ballooned to nearly $70 million with interest. Nearly all of it remained unpaid as of 2019. It is unlikely the families will see much more of the money owed to them.

For the families of Nicole Brown and Ronald Goldman, even the money would be no redemption. The person who killed their loved ones was still out there. And they believed without a doubt that person was O. J. Simpson. Speaking at the time of Simpson's parole, Fred Goldman expressed rage that Simpson was getting yet another chance to restart his life. There were no such chances for his son and Nicole Brown. "Ron doesn't get a second chance," he said.[6]

Simpson smiles in court after being granted parole in 2017.

# TIMELINE

## 1985

- O. J. Simpson marries Nicole Brown.

## 1992

- Brown files for divorce.

## 1994

- On June 12, Brown and her friend Ronald Goldman are found stabbed to death at Brown's condo in the Brentwood neighborhood of Los Angeles.
- In the early morning of June 13, Simpson arrives in Chicago, where he receives a call informing him his ex-wife has been killed. Simpson returns to Los Angeles and is questioned by police for several hours.
- On June 17, Simpson is charged with murder and a warrant is issued for his arrest. After failing to turn himself in, Simpson leads police on a low-speed chase across Los Angeles before being arrested at his home in Brentwood.
- On July 22, Simpson formally pleads not guilty.

## 1995

- On January 24, Simpson's murder trial begins.
- On October 3, Simpson is acquitted of both murder charges and goes free.

## 1996

- A civil trial begins in which the Goldman and Brown families sue Simpson for wrongful death.

## 1997

- A jury finds Simpson liable for the deaths of Brown and Goldman, awarding the victims' families a judgment of $33.5 million.

## 2006

- A book entitled *If I Did It* is proposed with Simpson's name as the author, detailing a hypothetical description of the murders. The book is scrapped, but the rights are later awarded to the Goldman family, who publishes it under a new title.

## 2007

- Simpson and five accomplices commit armed robbery while attempting to take back sports memorabilia that Simpson claims is his.

## 2008

- On October 3, Simpson is found guilty on 12 charges in relation to the robbery and sentenced to nine to 33 years in prison. Simpson serves his time at Lovelock Correctional Center in Nevada.

## 2017

- After serving the minimum of nine years, Simpson is released from prison on parole.

# ESSENTIAL FACTS

## SIGNIFICANT EVENTS

- When Nicole Brown Simpson and her friend Ronald Goldman were found stabbed to death at Brown's condo on June 12, 1994, suspicion immediately pointed to Brown's ex-husband O. J. Simpson, who had a history of domestic abuse and violent behavior. Simpson had no alibi for the time prosecutors believe the murders occurred.

- After a warrant was issued for Simpson's arrest, he failed to turn himself in and led police on a low-speed chase through Los Angeles on June 17. The chase ended when Simpson returned to his home, where he was arrested. Simpson was formally charged with murder, and his trial began the following January.

- During the trial, despite significant blood evidence and Simpson's history of domestic violence, the prosecution failed to make its case clear to the jury. The defense also raised questions of racism, including from within the Los Angeles Police Department and among some of the officers who investigated the case.

- The trial drew worldwide attention and was considered the "Trial of the Century." Simpson was acquitted of both murders on October 3, 1995.

## KEY PLAYERS

- O. J. Simpson was a former NFL running back who became an actor and celebrity spokesman in retirement. He was accused of murdering his ex-wife, Nicole Brown, in 1994. In a high-profile trial, Simpson was found not guilty of the murder. People have questioned the verdict ever since.

- Nicole Brown, the ex-wife of Simpson, was murdered at her home by an unknown killer at the age of 35 in 1994.

- Ronald Goldman, an aspiring actor and friend of Nicole Brown, was murdered alongside her in 1994. Simpson was accused but found not guilty of murdering Goldman as well.

- Marcia Clark was the lead prosecutor for the State of California and was assigned to the O. J. Simpson murder case, the highest-profile case of her career. After losing the case, Clark resigned from the Los Angeles County District Attorney's Office.

- Christopher Darden was another member of the prosecution team. He was famously responsible for asking Simpson to try on the bloody gloves at the trial, which did not fit.
- Johnnie Cochran was the lead defense attorney for Simpson. He had a reputation for being an experienced, charismatic attorney who advocated against racial injustice.

## IMPACT ON SOCIETY

The case was the top news story of 1995 and continues to be a point of fascination, with numerous films and TV shows made on the subject. Considered by many to be the "Trial of the Century," the case was one of the first major trials to utilize DNA evidence, which is now a common feature of criminal cases. As a double murder involving a beloved public figure, the Simpson case was widely covered and discussed, paving the way for sustained coverage of celebrity news and culture. The famous case also shed light on issues of domestic abuse and the role of race in the criminal justice system.

## QUOTE

"If it doesn't fit, you must acquit."

*—Defense attorney Johnnie Cochran, referring to O. J. Simpson's inability to put on the gloves found at the crime scene*

# GLOSSARY

**acquit**
To clear a person of the charges that have been brought against him or her.

**apolitical**
Having no involvement or interest in politics.

**convict**
To find a person guilty of criminal charges.

**displaced**
Relocated, often because of unexpected circumstances.

**district attorney**
The primary attorney in a jurisdiction tasked with prosecuting crimes.

**draft**
The process sports teams use to add new players to their teams.

**hypothetical**
Supposed or based on a theory rather than a reality.

**intercom**
An audio device for people to communicate across a house or property.

**liable**
To be bound or responsible according to law.

**memorabilia**
Items that are significant for historical reasons.

**mistrial**
When a trial has to be done over again for a certain reason or reasons.

**offensive line**
A group of football players whose job it is to block for other offensive players.

**parole**
Early release from prison because of good behavior under the condition that good behavior continue.

**point-blank**
At a close range.

**ratings**
The number of people watching a TV show.

**slurs**
Insults that are very severe.

**sterile**
Completely clean and free of impurities.

**warrant**
A document allowing law enforcement to carry out an arrest, a search, or an information-gathering operation.

# ADDITIONAL RESOURCES

## SELECTED BIBLIOGRAPHY


Anolik, Lili. "How O. J. Simpson Killed Popular Culture." *Vanity Fair*, 7 May 2014, vanityfair.com.

Dale, Maryclaire. "OJ Simpson Case Helped Bring Spousal Abuse Out of the Shadows." *Associated Press*, 12 June 2019, apnews.com.

Toobin, Jeffrey. *The Run of His Life: The People v. O.J. Simpson*. Random House, 2015.


## FURTHER READINGS

Burling, Alexis. *Race in the Criminal Justice System*. Abdo, 2018.

Carmichael, L. E. *Forensic Science: In Pursuit of Justice*. Abdo, 2015.

Hunt, Amber, and Emily G. Thompson. *Unsolved Murders: True Crime Cases Uncovered*. DK, 2019.

## ONLINE RESOURCES

To learn more about the O. J. Simpson murder case, please visit **abdobooklinks.com** or scan this QR code. These links are routinely monitored and updated to provide the most current information available.

## MORE INFORMATION

For more information on this subject, contact or visit the following organizations:

**ALCATRAZ EAST CRIME MUSEUM**

2757 Parkway
Pigeon Forge, TN 37863
865-453-3278
alcatrazeast.com

The Alcatraz East Crime Museum is home to Al Cowlings's white Ford Bronco used in the low-speed chase on June 17, 1994.

**THE O.J. TOUR**

Brentwood
Los Angeles, CA 90049
310-614-4163
theojtour.com

The O.J. Tour takes passengers in a white Ford Bronco to several key locations from the case and trial, including Nicole Brown's condo and the site of the restaurant where Ronald Goldman worked.

**PRO FOOTBALL HALL OF FAME**

2121 George Halas Dr. NW
Canton, OH 44708
330-456-8207
profootballhof.com

Simpson is enshrined in the Pro Football Hall of Fame for his stellar NFL career.

# SOURCE NOTES


## CHAPTER 1. THE DOG WITH BLOODY PAWS

1. David Margolick. "Walking the Dog with Pablo Fenjves; Echoes of a Cry in the Night." *New York Times*, 22 Mar. 1995, nytimes.com. Accessed 30 Aug. 2019.

2. Nell Henderson. "Nicole Simpson's Neighbors Describe How Dog Led Them to Slaying Scene." *Washington Post*, 9 Feb. 1995, washingtonpost.com. Accessed 30 Aug. 2019.

3. Henderson, "Nicole Simpson's Neighbors Describe How Dog Led Them to Slaying Scene."

4. Anthony Crupi. "The Run of His Life: How Hertz and O. J. Simpson Changed Advertising." *Ad Age*, 14 June 2016, adage.com. Accessed 30 Aug. 2019.

5. "Detective: Simpson Asked No Questions When Told of Ex-Wife's Death." *CNN*, 29 Oct. 1996, cnn.com. Accessed 30 Aug. 2019.

6. "Bel Air Fire." *Los Angeles Fire Department Historical Society*, n.d., lafdmuseum.org. *Wayback Machine*, web.archive.org. Accessed 30 Aug. 2019.

## CHAPTER 2. O. J. ON THE RUN

1. Michael Fleeman. "AP Was There: OJ Simpson's Slow-Speed Chase." *San Diego Union-Tribune*, 10 June 2014, sandiegouniontribune.com. Accessed 30 Aug. 2019.

2. "O.J. Simpson's Suicide Letter before Ford Bronco Chase in 1994." *New York Daily News*, 12 June 2015, nydailynews.com. Accessed 30 Aug. 2019.

3. Cydney Adams. "June 17, 1994: O.J. Simpson White Bronco Chase Mesmerizes Nation." *CBS News*, 17 June 2016, cbsnews.com. Accessed 30 Aug. 2019.

4. Jeff Brazil. "O.C. Pair First to See Bronco, Call Police." *Los Angeles Times*, 19 June 1994, latimes.com. Accessed 30 Aug. 2019.

5. "Twenty Years Later: The Night O.J. Simpson's Bronco Chase Crashed the NBA Finals." *FOX Sports*, 17 June 2014, foxsports.com. Accessed 30 Aug. 2019.

6. "The 10 Busiest Interstates in the United States." *Hotshot Warriors*, 27 Mar. 2018, hotshotwarriors.com. Accessed 30 Aug. 2019.

7. Vincent Bugliosi. "Outrage: Five Reasons Why O.J. Simpson Got Away with Murder." *Washington Post*, 1996, washingtonpost.com. Accessed 30 Aug. 2019.

8. Jeffrey Toobin. *The Run of His Life: The People v. O.J. Simpson*. Random House, 2015. 219.

## CHAPTER 3. FOOTBALL AND MARRIAGE


1. Tim Cahill. "O.J. Simpson: A Man for Offseason." *Rolling Stone*, 8 Sept. 1977, rollingstone.com. Accessed 30 Aug. 2019.

2. "O.J. Simpson." *Pro Football Reference*, n.d., pro-football-reference.com. Accessed 30 Aug. 2019.

3. Dan Jenkins. "The Juice Is Turned On Again." *Sports Illustrated*, 13 Oct. 1975, si.com. Accessed 30 Aug. 2019.

4. "Running Back 'Juice' O.J. Simpson." *Pro Football Hall of Fame*, n.d., profootballhallof.com. Accessed 30 Aug. 2019.

5. Josh Meyer. "Police Records Detail 1989 Beating That Led to Charge." *Los Angeles Times*, 17 June 1994, latimes.com. Accessed 30 Aug. 2019.

6. Meyer, "Police Records Detail 1989 Beating That Led to Charge."

7. Meyer, "Police Records Detail 1989 Beating That Led to Charge."

8. "O.J. Simpson's Hall of Fame Speech (1985)." *Buffalo News*, 2 Aug. 2014, buffalonews.com. Accessed 30 Aug. 2019.

9. Sage Young. "Nicole Brown Simpson's 911 Calls Altered Public Perception of O.J. Simpson before His Trial Began." *Bustle*, 16 Feb. 2016, bustle.com. Accessed 30 Aug. 2019.

10. Maryclaire Dale. "O.J. Simpson Case Helped Bring Spousal Abuse Out of Shadows." *Associated Press*, 12 June 2019, apnews.com. Accessed 30 Aug. 2019.


## CHAPTER 4. THE ROLE OF RACE


1. "Watts Riots." *History*, 28 Sept. 2017, history.com. Accessed 30 Aug. 2019.

2. "Watts Riots."

3. "Watts Riots."

4. Larry Altman. "Chokeholds Have Been Banned in Los Angeles for Decades." *Daily Breeze*, 4 Dec. 2014, dailybreeze.com. Accessed 30 Aug. 2019.

5. John L. Mitchell. "The Raid That Still Haunts L.A." *Los Angeles Times*, 14 March 2001, latimes.com. Accessed 30 Aug. 2019.

6. "Los Angeles Riots." *History*, 18 Apr. 2017, history.com. Accessed 30 Aug. 2019.

7. Ralph Wiley. "White Lies: HBO Gets It Half Right." *ESPN Page 2*, n.d., espn.com/page2. Accessed 30 Aug. 2019.

8. "Census Data: Output for Los Angeles City, CA." *State of the Cities Data Systems*, n.d., socds.huduser.gov. Accessed 30 Aug. 2019.

9. Isabel Wilkerson. "Whose Side to Take: Women, Outrage and the Verdict on O.J. Simpson." *New York Times*, 8 Oct. 1995, nytimes.com. Accessed 30 Aug. 2019.

10. Isabel Wilkerson, "Whose Side to Take: Women, Outrage and the Verdict on O.J. Simpson."

11. Eudie Pak. "O.J. Simpson: The Key Players in His Murder Trial." *Biography*, 11 Apr. 2019, biography.com. Accessed 30 Aug. 2019.

# SOURCE NOTES CONTINUED

## CHAPTER 5. THE TRIAL BEGINS

1. "The O.J. Simpson Murder Trial: Excerpts of Opening Statements by Simpson Prosecutors." *Los Angeles Times*, 25 Jan. 1995, latimes.com. Accessed 30 Aug. 2019.

2. David Margolick. "As Simpson Trial Opens, State Tells Jury of Long Blood Trail." *New York Times*, 25 Jan. 1995. Accessed 30 Aug. 2019.

3. Sheena Butler-Young. "The Real Story behind the Infamous O.J. Simpson Shoes." *Footwear News*, 6 Apr. 2016, footwearnews.com. Accessed 5 Sept. 2019.

4. "Putting DNA to Work." *Virtual Koshland Science Museum*, n.d., koshland-science-museum.org. Accessed 30 Aug. 2019.

## CHAPTER 6. THE GLOVE DOESN'T FIT

1. Thomas L. Jones. "O. J. Simpson: Time to Go Home." *TruTV*, n.d., trutv.com. *Wayback Machine*, web.archive.org. Accessed 30 Aug. 2019.

2. "Forensics at the OJ Simpson Trial." *Crime Museum*, n.d., crimemuseum.org. Accessed 30 Aug. 2019.

3. Matt Young. "The Story behind OJ Simpson's Infamous Gloves: Did They Fit, or Not?" *News.com.au*, 19 Apr. 2016, news.com.au. Accessed 30 Aug. 2019.

## CHAPTER 7. THE VERDICT

1. Nicole Jones. "The People v. O.J. Simpson Recap: Episode 8 Fact Check." *Vanity Fair*, 23 Mar. 2016, vanityfair.com. Accessed 30 Aug. 2019.

2. "Super Bowl Ratings History (1967–Present)." *Sports Media Watch*, n.d., sportsmediawatch.com. Accessed 30 Aug. 2019.

3. Pamela Engel. "America Came to a Standstill during the O.J. Verdict – Here's Everything That Stopped." *Business Insider*, 12 June 2014, businessinsider.com. Accessed 30 Aug. 2019.

4. Jim Newton. "Simpson Not Guilty: Drama Ends 474 Days after Arrest." *Los Angeles Times*, 4 Oct. 1995, latimes.com. Accessed 30 Aug. 2019.

5. CNN. "(Raw) 1995: O.J. Simpson Verdict Is Not Guilty." *YouTube*, 9 June 2014, youtube.com. Accessed 30 Aug. 2019.

6. CNN, "(Raw) 1995: O.J. Simpson Verdict Is Not Guilty."

7. Newton, "Simpson Not Guilty."

8. Newton, "Simpson Not Guilty."

9. Newton, "Simpson Not Guilty."

10. Newton, "Simpson Not Guilty."

11. "Jurors Say Evidence Made the Case for Simpson." *CNN*, 4 Oct. 1995, cnn.com. Accessed 30 Aug. 2019.

12. Char Adams. "'You Were Right': Robert Shapiro Finally Reveals What O.J. Simpson Whispered to Him after Acquittal." *People*, 18 May 2016, people.com. Accessed 30 Aug. 2019.

13. Gallup, CNN, and USA Today. "The O. J. Simpson Trial: Opinion Polls." *Famous Trials*, 1995, famous-trials.com. Accessed 30 Aug. 2019.

14. Matt Bonesteel. "A History Lesson for the Kids: Why the O.J. Simpson Trial Was Such a Big Deal." *Washington Post*, 4 Mar. 2016, washingtonpost.com. Accessed 30 Aug. 2019.

## CHAPTER 8. THE LAWSUIT


1. Dominick Dunne. "O.J. Simpson: Life after the Murder Trial." *Vanity Fair*, December 1995, vanityfair.com. Accessed 30 Aug. 2019.

2. Alan Abrahamson. "Simpson Expands on Slaying Remark Made to Magazine." *Los Angeles Times*, 17 Jan. 1998, latimes.com. Accessed 30 Aug. 2019.

3. Abrahamson, "Simpson Expands on Slaying Remark."

4. "New Owner Demolishes O.J. Simpson Mansion." *Chicago Tribune*, 30 July 1998, chicagotribune.com. Accessed 30 Aug. 2019.


## CHAPTER 9. SIMPSON GOES TO PRISON


1. Erin McClam. "Publisher Calls Book O.J.'s 'Confession.'" *Spokesman-Review*, 15 Nov. 2006, spokesmanreview.com. *WebCite*, webcitation.org. Accessed 30 Aug. 2019.

2. Anjelica Oswald. "How OJ Simpson Says He Would've Murdered Nicole Brown and Ron Goldman – 'If' He Did It." *Business Insider*, 5 Feb. 2016, businessinsider.com. Accessed 30 Aug. 2019.

3. Celia Walden. "O.J. Simpson Prosecutor: 'His Murder Trial Ruined My Life – But 20 Years On, I'm Back." *Telegraph*, 18 Mar. 2016, telegraph.co.uk. Accessed 30 Aug. 2019.

4. "Murdoch Cancels OJ Simpson Plans." *BBC News*, 21 Nov. 2006, news.bbc.co.uk. Accessed 30 Aug. 2019.

5. Kevin Fallon. "Remember When O.J. Simpson Had a Prank Show Called 'Juiced'?" *Daily Beast*, 28 Jan. 2016, thedailybeast.com. Accessed 30 Aug. 2019.

6. Amanda Holpuch. "OJ Simpson Granted Parole after Serving Nine Years of Robbery Sentence." *Guardian*, 20 July 2017, theguardian.com. Accessed 30 Aug. 2019.

# INDEX

*Ad Age*, 11
Akita dog breed, 4–6, 9–10, 52, 86

Bel Air Fire, 12
Bloomingdale's, 54, 66
Boztepe, Sukru, 6–7
Brady, Tom, 12
Brown, James, 47
Brown, Nicole, 9–12, 13, 14, 23, 29–33, 42, 48–53, 58, 62, 65, 66, 76, 78–82, 84, 86–91, 96

Chicago, Illinois, 9, 10, 11, 14–17, 21, 55, 57, 89
civil court, 78–83, 84, 91, 96
Clark, Marcia, 43–45, 53, 56, 66, 73, 89
Clinton, Bill, 70
Cochran, Johnnie, 47, 67, 71
conspiracy theories, 57, 64
Court TV, 50
Cowlings, Al "A. C.," 18–23, 74, 90

Darden, Christopher, 45, 48, 66–67, 73, 74
divorce, 9, 29, 33
DNA, 47, 55–57, 60–62, 65, 75
documentaries, 77, 95
domestic violence, 30–33, 43, 48–50, 81
Domino's pizza, 21

earthquakes, 7, 40
East Alcatraz Crime Museum, 22
Edwards, Harry, 41

Fenjves, Pablo, 4, 86
football, 7, 11, 16, 18–20, 24–29, 31, 43, 45, 83, 85, 92
  Buffalo Bills, 19, 27, 84
  college football, 19, 26–27, 43
  Heisman Trophy, 26, 85
  New England Patriots, 12
  Pro Football Hall of Fame, 31, 83
  San Francisco 49ers, 19, 27
  Super Bowl, 21, 70
Ford Bronco, 11, 18, 20–23, 52–53, 60, 70, 74, 77, 89, 92
Frye, Marquette, 34
Fuhrman, Mark, 62, 64–65, 68, 76
Fujisaki, Hiroshi, 80–81

Garcetti, Gil, 40–41
Gascon, David, 18
Gates, Daryl, 37, 39
Gilbert, Mike, 91–92
gloves, 10, 12, 53, 64–67, 73, 75, 81, 88
Goldman, Fred, 72–73, 96
Goldman, Ronald, 10, 12, 22, 51–54, 72, 74–75, 76, 78–80, 82, 89–91, 96
Gooding, Cuba, Jr., 95
Grier, Rosey, 60

Hertz, 11

*If I Did It*, 86–90
Ito, Lance, 58–60, 62, 68, 71

Jackson, Michael, 47
James, LeBron, 12

Kaelin, Kato, 7–8, 9, 12, 16, 50–51, 64, 88
Kardashian, Robert, 19
*Keeping Up with the Kardashians*, 19
King, Rodney, 38, 41, 64, 71

Lange, Thomas, 16
Las Vegas, Nevada, 91–92, 96
Los Angeles, California, 4, 9, 10, 12, 13, 14, 21, 22, 34–41, 64, 66, 70, 85
  Brentwood, 4, 12, 13, 22, 78
  Downtown, 4, 23, 40–41
  Hollywood, 4
  Watts, 34–36, 38
Los Angeles Police Department (LAPD), 14, 17–18, 34–39, 62–64, 71, 74, 76, 90
Love, Eulia, 36–37

Mays, Willie, 24–26
McKay, John, 19–20
memorabilia, 45, 85, 91–93
movies, 48, 77
Murdoch, Rupert, 90

NBA Finals, 21

Park, Allan, 8–9
Parker, William, 36
parole, 96
police brutality, 34–38, 43

Regan, Judith, 88
reporters, 14, 22
Riske, Robert, 9
robbery, 10, 90–93, 96

Santa Monica, California, 40–41, 81
Scheck, Barry, 61
Schwab, Steven, 4–6
Shapiro, Robert, 18, 45, 75
shoe prints, 16, 54, 57, 63, 81
Simpson, Jason, 23, 29, 57, 73, 84
Simpson, Jimmy, 26
Simpson, O. J., 7–12, 13, 14–23, 24–33, 36, 40–43, 44, 45–47, 48–57, 58–62, 64–67, 68, 71–77, 78–85, 86–96
Stanley Cup, 21

*Time* magazine, 42
*Tonight Show, The*, 62

University of Southern California (USC), 19, 26, 43

Vannatter, Philip, 12, 16

Whitley, Marguerite, 29, 84
World Cup, 21

# ABOUT THE AUTHOR

Todd Kortemeier is a sportswriter, editor, and children's book author based in Minnesota. He remembers watching the O. J. Simpson verdict on a classroom TV in third grade and has been fascinated by the case ever since. He and his wife live with their dachshund/beagle mix near Minneapolis.